Bookkeeping 2

Tutorial

David Cox
Michael Fardon

AAT WISE GUIDES – for convenient exam revision

This handy pocket-sized guide provides the **perfect study and revision resource** for the AAT Level 2 Certificate in Accounting.

available for:
Bookkeeping 1
Bookkeeping 2
Working in Accounting and Finance
Introduction to Costing

Visit www.osbornebooks.co.uk for further information and to place your order.

Published by Osborne Books Limited
Unit 1B Everoak Estate
Bromyard Road, Worcester WR2 5HP
Tel 01905 748071
Email books@osbornebooks.co.uk
Website www.osbornebooks.co.uk

Design by Laura Ingham

Printed by CPI Group (UK) Limited, Croydon, CR0 4YY, on environmentally friendly, acid-free paper from managed forests.

MIX
Paper from
responsible sources
FSC® C013604

British Library Cataloguing in Publication Data
A catalogue record for this book is available from the British Library

ISBN 978 1909173 040

Contents

Acknowledgements

The publisher wishes to thank the following for their help with the reading and production of the book: Maz Loton, Jon Moore and Cathy Turner. Thanks are also due to Debbie Board for her technical editorial work and to Laura Ingham for her designs for this series.

The publisher is indebted to the Association of Accounting Technicians for its help and advice to our authors and editors during the preparation of this text.

Authors

David Cox has more than twenty years' experience teaching accountancy students over a wide range of levels. Formerly with the Management and Professional Studies Department at Worcester College of Technology, he now lectures on a freelance basis and carries out educational consultancy work in accountancy studies. He is author and joint author of a number of textbooks in the areas of accounting, finance and banking.

Michael Fardon has extensive teaching experience of a wide range of banking, business and accountancy courses at Worcester College of Technology. He now specialises in writing business and financial texts and is General Editor at Osborne Books. He is also an educational consultant and has worked extensively in the areas of vocational business curriculum development.

Introduction

what this book covers

This book has been written specifically to cover the 'Control accounts, journals and the banking system' Unit which is mandatory for the revised (2013) AAT Level 2 Certificate in Accounting.

The book contains a clear text with worked examples and case studies, chapter summaries and key terms to help with revision. Each chapter has a wide range of activities, many in the style of the computer-based assessments used by AAT.

The book covers the areas of control accounts, journals and trial balance adjustments.

Bookkeeping 2 is a companion text to Osborne Books' *Bookkeeping 1* which covers the AAT Unit 'Processing bookkeeping transactions'.

Downloadable blank documents for use with this text are available in the Resources section of www.osbornebooks.co.uk.

Osborne Workbooks

Osborne Workbooks contain practice material which helps students achieve success in their assessments. *Bookkeeping 2 Workbook* contains a number of paper-based 'fill in' practice exams in the style of the computer-based assessment. Please visit www.osbornebooks.co.uk for further details and access to our online shop.

1 Banks, building societies and payment systems

this chapter covers...

This chapter is an introduction to the services and payment systems provided by banks and building societies in the UK.

The chapter describes:

- *the difference between banks and building societies (and particularly the smaller building societies)*
- *services offered by building societies*
- *services offered by the banks*

This chapter also introduces the following forms of payment and describes the various clearing systems where appropriate:

- *cash*
- *cheques*
- *plastic cards including credit cards, debit cards, prepayment cards and 'tap and go' cards*
- *direct payments using giro credits*
- *direct electronic payments, including BACS and Faster Payments*

This chapter also describes the policy adopted by the banks for storing documents and electronic data – all of which need to be kept safely and confidentially.

BANKS AND BUILDING SOCIETIES IN THE UK

what are banks and building societies?

The banking system in the UK fulfils the important function of accepting deposits and lending money. It basically 'oils the wheels' of the economy. It is made up of a wide variety of banks and a number of building societies.

- a **bank** is a limited company, owned by shareholders; well-known names include Barclays, HSBC and LloydsTSB
- a **building society** is a 'mutual' organisation owned by its members (ie its customers); well-known names include Nationwide (the biggest building society) and the smaller Yorkshire Building Society

The trend over the last few decades has been for the banks to 'buy out' building societies by paying the building society members (customers) sizeable sums of money or giving them shares in return for their ownership.

building societies – the services

The services offered by **building societies** are principally to the personal customer market rather than to businesses. These services include:

- deposits: current and savings accounts for the members (customers)
- loans: mortgages for house purchase

Larger building societies also provide property-linked business services. Nationwide, for example, organises finance for property projects, including major housing developments and schools. Smaller building societies, on the other hand, are not set up to deal with 'corporate' (ie business) services.

banks – the services

Banks have traditionally offered a wide range of services to both personal and business customers. If you work in a finance and accounting role in business you are most likely to be dealing with a bank. The main services they offer to businesses and other organisations include:

- current accounts – dealing with cash, cheques and automated payments
- deposit accounts – paying interest on surplus funds
- overdrafts – flexible borrowing on a current account to cover temporary requirements
- loan accounts – financing loans with flexible repayments
- mortgages – loans for property purchase

These business services are described in more detail on the next page.

banks and building societies – the difference

It is often difficult to tell the difference between banks and building societies in terms of the services they offer. For example Halifax and Santander are both banks whereas Nationwide is a building society. They all look very similar from the 'High Street.' The main difference is the **extra** services offered by the banks, for example:

- **business services**
- **specialised personal services** such as safe custody (looking after the valuables of personal customers), and wills and trusts

Both the banks and the larger building societies offer the same wide range of financial services expected by **personal customers**. These include:

- current accounts, debit cards, credit cards and other payment cards
- overdrafts, personal loans and mortgages
- insurance, travel money, investments

BANK SERVICES FOR THE BUSINESS CUSTOMER

business current account

A **business current account** is a 'working account' through which day-to-day financial transactions pass, including payments received from customers and payment of business expenses and wages.

Payments are made by cheque and also using the BACS (Bankers Automated Clearing Services) and the Faster Payments computer payment system to make electronic transfers. Regular statements are either sent by the bank in paper format to the business or are made available online.

A business can apply to the bank for an overdraft on the current account. This means that the business borrows on a temporary basis from the current account (see the next page).

deposit account

A **deposit account** is used for excess money held by a business, and interest is paid by the bank on the amount deposited. Current account facilities such as cheques, standing orders, direct debits, and overdrafts are not allowed on deposit accounts.

Many business customers have both a current and a deposit account. When money is needed on the current account it can be transferred from the deposit account by telephoned or online instructions.

Substantial sums of money (normally £500,000 plus) can be placed on deposit with a bank in what are often known as 'treasury accounts'. These accounts may allow withdrawals without notice, or they may need a longer period of notice of withdrawal, perhaps one month or three or six months.

overdraft

An **overdraft** is borrowing from the bank on a current account. If a business thinks it will need an overdraft, it should contact the bank and seek agreement for an overdraft 'facility' up to a certain limit for a specified time. Interest will be charged on overdrawn balances and an arrangement/renewal fee is normally payable. An overdraft is a very flexible arrangement because the customer can borrow when the need arises, and will only pay interest on the amount borrowed.

loan accounts

Whereas an overdraft is a means of borrowing on an ordinary current account and will cover day-to-day expenses of the business, loan accounts are long-term loans for long-term items, eg machinery and new projects. Some typical examples of loan account include:

business loan

A business loan is financing to cover large items of expense such as new machinery, premises expansion or a new project.

- loan amounts can range from £1,000 to £100,000
- interest is paid, either at a rate fixed at the beginning of the loan, or at a variable rate in line with market rates during the lifetime of the loan
- a bank loan is for a set time period, normally between 2 and 30 years
- the loan is often repaid in regular instalments, but this may be varied, for example with a 'repayment holiday' – this is where the borrower is allowed to wait a year or so before starting to make repayments; some loans can also be repaid in full at the end of the loan period

commercial mortgage

A commercial mortgage is a loan for up to twenty-five years to cover the purchase of property (the business equivalent of a 'home loan' mortgage to an individual).

- a mortgage is an arrangement in which property is used as security for borrowing; if the business defaults on the loan, the bank can sell the property to obtain the funds. Amounts range from £25,000 to £500,000
- banks can provide finance for the purchase of commercial property, normally up to 70% of its market value

■ interest is paid, either at a rate fixed at the beginning of the mortgage, or at a variable rate in line with market rates during the lifetime of the mortgage

other bank services for businesses

Banks operate a wide range of services for businesses. If you log onto the websites of the bigger banks, eg HSBC or LloydsTSB, you will see examples of these, including:

■ **debit and credit cards** and card payment processing – issuing company credit cards, processing card payments as a 'card merchant'

■ **insurance** – protection for business employees, premises and other risks

■ **international services** – currency accounts, overseas payments, dealing with exports and imports

Other (subsidiary) companies owned by the banks also help finance businesses through:

■ **leasing** – a leasing company buys an asset needed by the business and then 'rents' it out to the business (company cars, for example, are often leased rather than bought outright)

■ **factoring** – providing finance to companies against their invoices issued to customers; invoices are effectively 'bought' from the business that issues them and the factoring company then collects the money from the customer when the invoice is due

Bank services to businesses are summarised in the diagram below

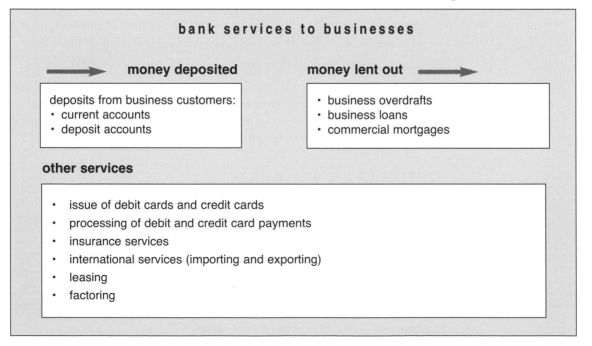

bank services to businesses

money deposited

deposits from business customers:
• current accounts
• deposit accounts

money lent out

• business overdrafts
• business loans
• commercial mortgages

other services

• issue of debit cards and credit cards
• processing of debit and credit card payments
• insurance services
• international services (importing and exporting)
• leasing
• factoring

The remainder of this chapter explains how the various methods of payment work in practice and how they are 'cleared' – ie processed – through the banking system. Later in this book we describe the ways in which payments received by a business and payments made by a business are checked and validated and security procedures are followed (see Chapters 2 and 3).

CASH

Some businesses, shops for example, take cash – notes and coins – in payment for goods and services. They do not, however, use cash as a means of transferring money through the banking system as it is obviously too bulky, a security risk and impractical.

Cash is still one of the simplest methods of making payment for goods and services, particularly where small amounts are involved. However, the suggestion that the 'cashless society' is growing has been given support with the introduction of the 'tap and go' card: this is a plastic debit card which is used to make purchases of under £20 just by 'tapping' a retailer terminal and deducting the amount from the customer's bank account (see page 12).

The areas where the banks can help businesses with cash include:

■ cash paid into their accounts over the counter with a paying-in slip (see below)

■ they provide cash when a business needs to pay cash wages

■ the night safe facility allows a business to lodge cash in a special wallet which is placed in a special secure 'letter box' in the wall of the bank outside normal banking hours

a paying in slip showing cash and cheques being paid in

CHEQUES

Cheques are issued by banks and building societies to their current account customers. Payment by cheque used to be in common use by businesses and personal customers, but is now declining – in fact, some large retail stores now refuse to take cheques. They are still popular, however, for payments made by post, eg payment of bills and payment by business customers who have bought goods and services on credit from businesses. A specimen cheque is shown at the bottom of this page.

what is a cheque?

A cheque is an order in writing and signed by the customer (the 'drawer') telling a bank to pay an amount to someone (the 'payee').

Although some organisations now print out their cheques on computer systems, a large number of cheques used in business are still written by hand. Great care must be taken both when writing out cheques and also when receiving written cheques in payment; they must be checked and examined to ensure that all the details and signatures are correct. If they are not correct in this way they may be invalid.

Note the use of the terms 'payee' and 'drawer' on the cheque shown below.

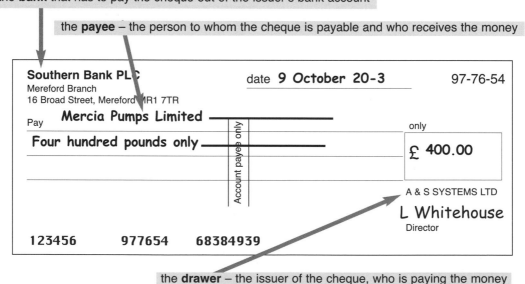

the **bank** that has to pay the cheque out of the issuer's bank account

the **payee** – the person to whom the cheque is payable and who receives the money

the **drawer** – the issuer of the cheque, who is paying the money

the 'parties' to a cheque – the people involved

issuing of cheques

When writing out (using ink, not pencil) or printing out the cheque you should take care to complete the following details:

- correct date
- name of the payee (person receiving the money)
- amount in words
- amount in figures (which should be the same as the amount in words)
- authorised signature (it may be that of a line manager)
- counterfoil (date, amount, payee)

No room should be left on the cheque for possible fraudulent additions or alterations; any blank spaces should be ruled through with a single line. If any errors are made when you are writing out the cheque, they should be corrected and an authorised signature placed close to the alteration in order to tell the bank that it is an approved correction.

computer cheque printing

Computer cheque printing is increasingly used by organisations which use computer accounting programs. The computer will automatically indicate payments that are due and, subject to authorisation, print out the remittance advice and cheque together, ready for posting. The computer involved must be closely controlled – and probably password protected – in order to prevent unauthorised access and fraudulent payments.

CHEQUE CLEARING

Every working day cheques are paid into banks and building societies. These cheques are then passed on to the banks of the people and organisations that issued them so that the cheques can be authorised for payment. This process is known as the 'cheque clearing' and a cheque which has been authorised and paid is said to have 'cleared'. Note that cheques paid into building societies are also passed on through this bank clearing system. In other words, **all cheques** pass through the bank clearing system.

If authorisation is not given by the issuer's bank, usually because the issuer of the cheque has not got the money on the account, the cheque will 'bounce' and will be sent back to the bank where it was paid in and the money will be deducted from the account. This is known as a **dishonoured cheque**.

The problem with this old-fashioned cheque clearing system is that a customer paying in a cheque may not know:

- when the cheque might start to earn interest (if the account pays interest)
- when they can draw out the money that they have paid in
- whether or not the cheque has 'bounced'(returned) – in which case the money will not be available

The '2-4-6' clearance cycle was introduced to sort out these uncertainties.

the 2-4-6 clearance cycle

The numbers in the '2-4-6' clearance cycle refer to the number of working days after paying in a cheque that:

- interest may be paid on the amount paid in (if it is an account that pays interest)
- customers can withdraw the amount paid in
- customers can be absolutely certain that the money is safe in their account and the cheque will not be 'bounced' (returned) and the money taken out again

The actual number of days in each case is calculated as shown below.

Note that 'days' means working days – ie excluding Saturdays, Sundays and bank holidays.

- after **2** working days interest may be paid on the amount paid in

- after **4** working days the amount can be withdrawn from the account

- after **6** working days the money paid in is guaranteed safe and cannot be deducted by the bank from the account if the cheque has bounced

There is sometimes confusion about how these 'working days' tie up with the day on which the cheque was paid in. The answer is that the day on which the cheque was paid in **is not counted** as one of the working days.

This can be illustrated using a specific example:

■ Ben banks at RBS (Nottingham branch). On **Monday** he pays into the RBS branch a £500 Barclays (Liverpool branch) cheque issued by Tom.

  The cheque is sent off in the cheque clearing by RBS to Barclays (Liverpool) on **Monday**.

■ Ben can expect interest to be paid on this £500 (if the account pays interest) **2** working days later, ie on **Wednesday** (Monday + 2 days).

■ Ben can withdraw this £500 from the account **4** working days later, ie on **Friday** (Monday + 4 days) but still runs the risk of the cheque being bounced and losing his money.

■ Ben can withdraw this £500 from the account **6** working days later, ie by the end of **the following Tuesday** (Monday + 6 working days) and know that the cheque will not bounce and the money cannot be taken off his account.

Now study this process in the diagram below.

the 2-4-6 clearance cycle		
actual day	**working day number**	**stage in the clearance cycle**
Monday	0	the cheque for £500 is paid in and sent off for clearing
Tuesday	1	
Wednesday	2	interest on the £500 may be paid on the account
Thursday	3	
Friday	4	the £500 can be withdrawn, but at the risk of the cheque bouncing and the money being deducted from the account
Saturday Sunday	*It's the weekend – not counted as working days*	
Monday	5	
Tuesday	6	at the end of this day the £500 will be safe and the cheque cannot bounce

PAYMENT BY PLASTIC CARD

There are a number of types of plastic cards commonly used as a means of payment. They include:

- **debit cards** - where payment is taken straight from the bank account of the customer
- **credit cards** - where payment is made by the customer to the credit card issuer at a later date than the purchase
- **prepayment cards** - where a customer has already 'topped up' (prepaid) the card up to a certain value and payment is taken from that value

The electronic methods used to process the payments for these cards include:

- 'Chip and PIN' technology where the customer enters a PIN (Personal Identification Number) on a terminal
- radio technology where the card details are transferred to the terminal by 'tapping' or swiping the card
- a terminal or web link where the customer is not present and the transaction is a mail order or online purchase, processed remotely using the card details provided by the customer

debit cards

Debit cards enable bank and building societies customers to make payments from their bank accounts electronically when they make purchases.

A debit card has the obvious advantages of being quick and convenient to use. Debit cards issuers include Visa and Maestro. It normally takes up to two days for the amount of a purchase to be taken from the account. Debit cards are also used for cash withdrawals.

'tap and go' cards

Radio technology has made possible the '**Tap and Go**' debit cards, for example the Mastercard PayPass, where a simple tap on the terminal at the checkout (in shops and public transport) makes it possible to pay for items under £20 and deduct the money from the buyer's account.

credit cards

Credit cards provide a means of obtaining goods and services immediately, but paying for them later. Examples include Visa and Mastercard.

Credit cards are issued to customers of banks, building societies, shops and a wide variety of businesses and other organisations. Goods and services can be obtained at shops and other outlets having computer terminals. Credit cards can also be used for mail order, telephoned and internet sales.

Sellers of goods and services use a **card merchant** to process all their card payments, and pay a set percentage (up to 5%) of each transaction amount for the use of the credit card facility.

Each month the cardholder is provided with a paper or online statement of the purchases made in the previous month and can choose to pay off by a set monthly date the full balance of the account, or to pay part only, carrying forward the remaining balance to the next month. Payment can be made by cheque or direct debit. Interest is charged on any balance still owing to the credit card company after the monthly payment date. An annual flat fee may be charged to the cardholder for the use of the card.

prepayment cards

Prepayment cards are becoming increasingly popular. They have the same appearance as debit or credit cards, but there is a major difference: they are purchased by the customer and have a preloaded 'balance to spend'. They can be disposable or they can be topped up at a bank, Post Office or PayPoint terminal. They work on the same principle as an Oyster Card on the London transport system. Prepayment cards:

- can be used for making shop or online purchases, and withdrawing cash – but only up to the limit on the card
- are useful for customers who cannot obtain a credit card for personal credit reasons (eg poor credit record), and for people under 18 who do not qualify for a credit card
- can be used internationally.

For businesses receiving payment, prepayment cards are dealt with in the same way as a debit or credit card. There is no clearing cycle for the cards because payment is made in advance.

BANK GIRO CREDITS

We have already seen earlier in this chapter (page 7) how money can be paid into a bank account by means of a bank paying-in slip. The banking system also allows for a **bank giro credit** to be paid in at one branch and processed through a **three day clearing system** to another bank or branch. The bank credit clearing system is used for paying bills (eg electricity, gas, telephone) and settling credit card accounts.

The preprinted bank giro credit is usually a tear-off slip at the bottom of a bill. The person or business paying the bill will fill in:

■ the amount of the payment

■ the date that the payment is being made at the bank

■ in some cases the signature of the person paying in the credit at the bank

The bill is then taken to the bank and paid in, together with a cheque for the appropriate amount. A water bill is shown below, together with the cheque used to pay the bill.

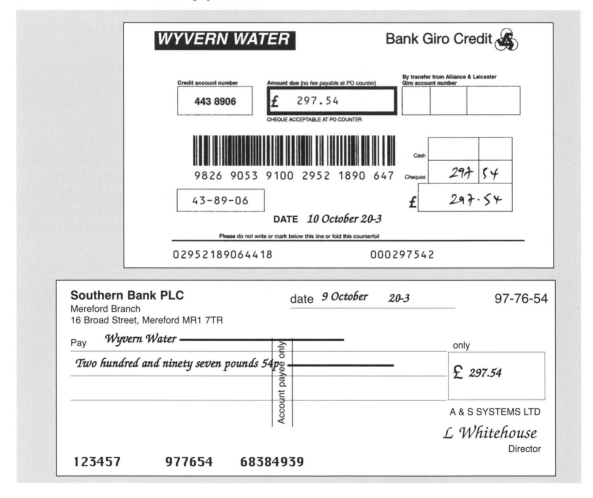

ELECTRONIC PAYMENTS BY COMPUTER

BACS system

Bankers Automated Clearing Services (BACS) is a computer transfer payment system owned by the banks. It is widely used for regular payments such as insurance premiums, settlement of trade debts, wages and salaries.

BACS is a cheap and efficient means of payment because, instead of a piece of paper having to be prepared and despatched, the transfer is set up on a computer file and transferred between the banks' computers – the payment goes direct from account to account and takes three working days.

BACS direct credits

Businesses often need to make regular payments of **variable** amounts, eg:

- paying wages on pay day
- making payments to established suppliers at the end of each month

The banks have established a BACS **direct credit** system to process these variable payments. Whenever the payments are due to be paid the business sends the bank a schedule (faxed or sent electronically) setting out the details of the payments. **The payment cycle is three working days.** If a business wants its suppliers or employees to have the money in their accounts on Friday, the money must leave the business's account on Wednesday.

Faster Payments

Faster Payments enables customers to send **same-day** payments from their account to another account at a bank or building society which participates in the scheme. Features of the service include:

- customer instructions for payment may be given at the bank branch, by telephone or over the internet
- customer instructions include the name of the account to receive the payment, the account number, the sort code and any identifying reference number
- the customer must have enough money in the account for the payment
- the payment will normally take only **two hours** to reach its destination account; once the payment has been sent it cannot be cancelled
- the bank sending the payment will receive an acknowledgement that the payment has been made when it reaches its destination account; if there is a problem with the payment at the receiving bank it will be rejected and the sending bank will be notified

standing orders

The business that needs to make **regular payments of the same amount**, eg a loan repayment, completes a written authority instructing the bank what payments to make, to whom, and when. The bank then sets up the instructions on its computer, and the payments are made automatically by computer link:

- using **BACS** – with a three working day payment cycle
- using **Faster Payments** – with a same day payment cycle

BACS direct debits

The direct debit system is useful for organisations such as insurance companies that receive a large number of variable payments:

- direct debits can be used for either fixed and variable amounts and/or where the time intervals between payments vary
- it is the business that receives payment that prepares the computer instructions requesting the payer's bank account for payment through the banking system

mobile electronic payments – future developments

The most significant current development in payment technology is the establishment by the main UK banks through the Payments Council of a database which will allow owners of smartphones to:

- download an app from their bank (eg Barclays, who already offer PingIt)
- enter a PIN number or password to log on to the app
- choose the recipient (who must also have an app downloaded from their bank) and select the recipient's phone number
- enter an amount to pay, and confirm the payment transaction

The payment will then be made as a Faster Payments transfer. It is expected that this will prove very popular with customers and small businesses.

'ONE-OFF' LARGE PAYMENTS

Businesses can make 'one-off' payments using the bank CHAPS system or by issuing bank drafts.

CHAPS

CHAPS (Clearing House Automated Payments System) is used for high value same-day payments sent by the banks through their computer networks. CHAPS is used extensively by solicitors when they are arranging the purchase and sale of property for clients. CHAPS payments cannot be cancelled after they have been sent.

bank drafts

An organisation may have to make a large purchase – for example new vehicles – and be asked to pay by bank draft. A bank draft is a cheque written out by a bank. It is a guaranteed means of payment which is as good as cash, but without the security risks that cash involves. Note that a bank draft cannot be cancelled or stopped once it has been issued, but if it is a forged bank draft it is worthless. Seller beware!

PAYMENT CYCLES AND THE BANK BALANCE

It is important to know the payment cycles for different types of payment (eg cheque, BACS, Faster Payments) because they will affect:

■ for a **payment received** – the date that the money will be cleared on the bank account and can be used for payments or for earning interest

■ for a **payment made** – the date that the payment will leave the bank account and so reduce the amount of money available

The 2-4-6 cheque clearance, for example (see pages 10-11) means that if you pay in a cheque for £1,000 you will have to wait four working days for it to 'clear' and be able to use the £1,000 for making a payment. If, however, you send a cheque to a supplier, it will be a number of days before it is deducted from your account (ie time taken in the post and the clearance time) and you would be able to rely on the funds being available for that time.

If, on the other hand, you receive a BACS or Faster Payment transfer to your account, the money will be 'cleared' and made available on the same day so that you can make a payment straightaway.

RETENTION OF BANKING DOCUMENTS

filing retention policy

Over the years organisations are likely to accumulate a large volume of paper-based documents, including bank documents, for example paying-in books and cheque book counterfoils and bank statements. All organisations normally have a **retention policy** stating that records are normally kept for **six years, plus the current year**.

The reasons for this are legal requirements. Legislation covering company law, taxation and data protection generally requires that records should be kept for anywhere between three and six years.

destruction of filing records

Any business should always keep its records secure and so that no unauthorised person can get hold of confidential information. This is particularly important because if fraudsters get hold of customer credit card details and bank account numbers, they can also get hold of money from customers' accounts. After the six years has elapsed these records should be destroyed or shredded (paper records), or 'wiped' (data held electronically). This includes the wiping or destruction of a computer's hard disk if a computer is being replaced.

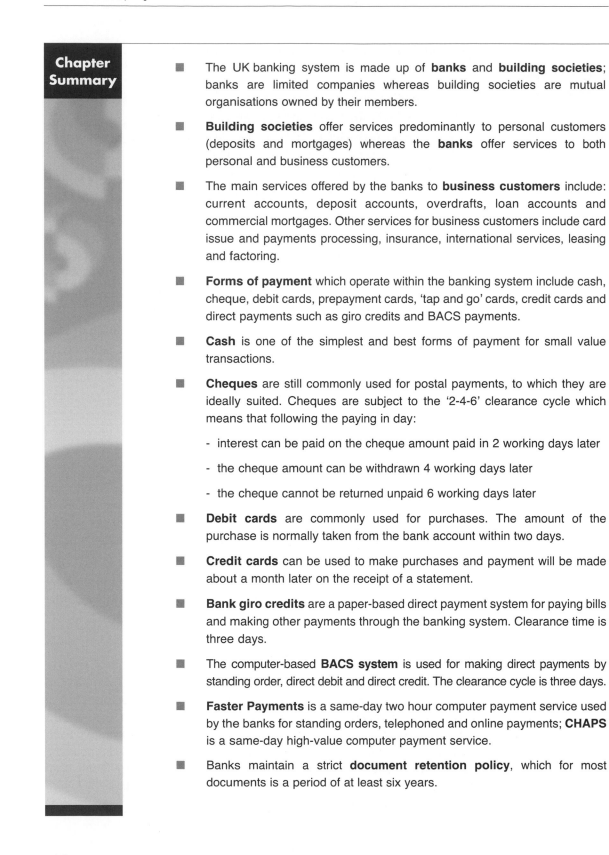

Chapter Summary

- The UK banking system is made up of **banks** and **building societies**; banks are limited companies whereas building societies are mutual organisations owned by their members.

- **Building societies** offer services predominantly to personal customers (deposits and mortgages) whereas the **banks** offer services to both personal and business customers.

- The main services offered by the banks to **business customers** include: current accounts, deposit accounts, overdrafts, loan accounts and commercial mortgages. Other services for business customers include card issue and payments processing, insurance, international services, leasing and factoring.

- **Forms of payment** which operate within the banking system include cash, cheque, debit cards, prepayment cards, 'tap and go' cards, credit cards and direct payments such as giro credits and BACS payments.

- **Cash** is one of the simplest and best forms of payment for small value transactions.

- **Cheques** are still commonly used for postal payments, to which they are ideally suited. Cheques are subject to the '2-4-6' clearance cycle which means that following the paying in day:

  - interest can be paid on the cheque amount paid in 2 working days later

  - the cheque amount can be withdrawn 4 working days later

  - the cheque cannot be returned unpaid 6 working days later

- **Debit cards** are commonly used for purchases. The amount of the purchase is normally taken from the bank account within two days.

- **Credit cards** can be used to make purchases and payment will be made about a month later on the receipt of a statement.

- **Bank giro credits** are a paper-based direct payment system for paying bills and making other payments through the banking system. Clearance time is three days.

- The computer-based **BACS system** is used for making direct payments by standing order, direct debit and direct credit. The clearance cycle is three days.

- **Faster Payments** is a same-day two hour computer payment service used by the banks for standing orders, telephoned and online payments; **CHAPS** is a same-day high-value computer payment service.

- Banks maintain a strict **document retention policy**, which for most documents is a period of at least six years.

Key Terms		
	current account	an account which is used for day-to-day payments
	deposit account	an account which pays interest and is used for savings and surplus money
	overdraft	a current account from which a customer may borrow from time to time
	business loan	a long-term loan with an agreed repayment programme, used for financing a business
	commercial mortgage	a long-term loan to finance the purchase of property
	cheque	a written instruction to a bank by a customer (the drawer) to pay a specified amount of money to a specified person (the payee) – clearance using the 2-4-6 day cycle (see Chapter Summary)
	debit card	a card issued to a customer which can be used for purchases and cash withdrawals; payment is taken from the account within two days
	credit card	a card issued to a customer on a 'buy now and pay later' basis; payment is made on receipt of a statement
	prepayment card	a card which can be purchased and given a 'balance to spend' – useful when the customer is under 18
	bank giro credit	a paper-based direct payment through the banking system with a three day clearance cycle
	BACS	Bankers Automated Clearing Services – a three day computer-based direct payment system
	BACS direct credit	direct BACS payments – with a three day clearance
	standing order	regular BACS payments, set up with the bank by the customer paying the amounts
	direct debit	regular and variable BACS payments, set up by the organisation receiving the payments
	Faster Payments	same day payments (usually 2 hours) between banks and building societies – instructions normally given by telephone or online
	CHAPS	high value, same day, payments sent through the banks' computer systems
	bank draft	a cheque written out by a bank – as good as cash – used for high value purchases

Activities

1.1   A building society is set up as:

(a)   a public limited company owned by shareholders

(b)   a mutual organisation owned by its customers

Which one of these options is correct?

1.2   Select THREE services most likely to be offered by the smaller Building Societies from the list below, indicating your answer by ticking the appropriate boxes.

	✔
Commercial loan	
Regular savings account	
Wills and trusts	
Insurance	
Credit cards	
Safe custody of valuables	

1.3   An overdraft:

(a)   is only available to business customers

(b)   is only available to personal customers

(c)   is available to both business and personal customers

(d)   is repayable in fixed instalments

(e)   is charged a fixed amount of interest each month

(f)   is only charged interest on the amounts borrowed each month

Which two of these options are correct?

1.4   A cheque is:

(a)   an instruction to a customer to pay to the bank a specific amount of money

(b)   an instruction to a bank to pay to a specified person a specific amount of money

(c)   an instruction to a specified person to pay a specific amount of money

Which one of these options is correct?

1.5   The bank cheque clearing is called the 2-4-6 system because the numbers relate to the number of working days after the cheque is cleared that:

(a)   the customer can withdraw the money amount of the cheque

(b)   the cheque is guaranteed not to be returned ('bounced')

(c)   interest can be paid (if applicable) on the amount of the cheque paid in

You are to state which of the three numbers (2-4-6) applies to statements (a), (b) and (c).

1.6   A 'Chip and PIN' debit card can be used to make a purchase through a shop terminal even if there is not enough money available in the account of the cardholder.

True or false?

1.7   A credit card allows payment:

(a)   of the full amount by the given date and no interest will be payable

(b)   of the minimum amount by the given date and no interest will be payable

(c)   whenever the cardholder wants and interest will be payable straightaway

Which one of these options is correct?

1.8   A bank giro credit is:

(a)   an online direct payment which is used to pay variable amounts owing

(b)   a paper-based direct payment which is used to pay variable amounts owing

(c)   a computer-based direct payment which is used to pay variable amounts owing

Which one of these options is correct?

1.9   Which plastic card requires the card holder to pay for purchase transactions in advance?

(a)   a credit card

(b)   a debit card

(c)   a prepayment card

Which one of these options is correct?

1.10   BACS standing orders are best suited for payments which:

(a)   are equal in amount

(b)   are variable in amount

(c)   are made on different dates in the month

Which one of these options is correct?

1.11   CHAPS stands for:

(a)   Cheque Handling Automated Payments System

(b)   Clearing House Automated Payments System

(c)   Clearing House Advanced Payment System

Which one of these options is correct?

1.12   The Faster Payments Service normally makes payment to the account in:

(a)   two minutes

(b)   two hours

(c)   two days

Which one of these options is correct?

1.13   The document retention policy of a bank is normally for a period of:

(a)   six months

(b)   six years

(c)   ten years

Which one of these options is correct?

1.14 You are running a business and need to make various payments each month. Which method of payment from the list provided at the end of the question would you choose as the best to use in the following situations:

(a)   paying variable amounts to twenty suppliers at the end of each month

(b)   paying a monthly rates bill of twelve fixed instalments of £258.90

(c)   buying a new car costing £34,000 for the finance director

(d)   settling an electricity bill which has variable quarterly payments

(e)   buying a jar of coffee for office use from the local foodstore

(f)   paying £350,000 to a firm of solicitors for the purchase of a new shop

List of possible means of payment:

1   standing order

2   cash which you can claim back from the person who operates the petty cash

3   bank draft

4   direct debit

5   CHAPS payment

6   BACS direct credit

2 Making payments

this chapter covers...

The last chapter described the different types of payment made by organisations. This chapter explains in more detail the procedures for making payments by a business settling expenses and paying its suppliers.

The chapter sets out the steps followed to make sure that payments are authorised and that confidentiality is maintained. The chapter covers the specific areas of:

■ making payments by cheque

■ making payments by giro credit inter-bank transfer (paper-based)

■ making payments by BACS inter-bank transfer or Faster Payments (computer-based):

- standing orders

- direct credits

- direct debits

■ company credit cards

■ online banking

OUTGOING PAYMENTS

Payments can be made by cheque, electronically or by cash (less common):

issue of cheques

- paying suppliers by cheque for goods and services provided
- paying for 'one-off' items of **capital** expenditure, eg a computer system
- paying bills by cheque and bank giro transfer

paying by electronic transfer

- paying wages
- paying suppliers for goods and services
- paying bills

PAYING TRADE SUPPLIERS

internal procedures

Each business or organisation will have its own policies and regulations laid down to ensure that payments to suppliers of goods and services are only made when the goods and services have been received as ordered. A supplier of goods and services is paid when:

- the documents relating to the transaction – the purchase order, delivery note (or goods received note) and invoice have been checked against each other (they are normally filed together)
- any credit due, eg for returned goods, has been received in the form of a credit note
- all discounts, whether **settlement (cash) discount** (for early payment) or **trade discount** or **bulk discount** have been identified and allowed for
- the payment has received the necessary authorisation – often in the form of a manager's initials on the invoice, or a rubber stamp

timescales – when to pay?

Each business will also have its own policies and regulations dictating *when* payment is to be made.

payment on invoice – diary system

Businesses sometimes pay strictly according to the due date of the invoice. Each invoice (and all the accompanying documentation), when it is received will be marked with the due date of payment – eg 30 days after the invoice issue date – and placed in a diary system. With this system a business may make individual payments to different suppliers on any number of days of the month. The system is best suited to small businesses which do not have too many payments to make.

payment runs – based on statements

Another widely adopted system is for suppliers to be paid regularly on the basis of the monthly statement issued rather than in response to individual invoices. A business using this system will set up **payment runs** – ie days on which payments will be made during the month, for example once a month on the last day of the month. On each payment run date the supplier statements will be examined and outstanding items paid (unless they are disputed). Payments are often set out on a schedule, authorised by a line manager.

REMITTANCE ADVICES

A **remittance advice** lists the invoices that are being paid and the credit notes that are being deducted. Payment can be made by **cheque**, in which case the remittance advice accompanies the payment, or electronically by **BACS** or **Faster Payments**, in which case the remittance advice is sent separately by post, fax, or by email

paying by cheque

If you are paying a supplier you should attach the cheque to the remittance advice. This may be a tear-off slip attached to the supplier's statement of account, or it may be a standard form as illustrated below.

TO	REMITTANCE ADVICE	FROM
Cool Socks Limited Unit 45 Elgar Estate, Broadfield, BR7 4ER	8 December 20-3	**Vogue Ltd** 56 Shaftesbury Road Manorfield MA1 6GP

date	your reference	our reference	payment amount
03 11 –3	INVOICE 788106	876213	500.00
15 11 –3	INVOICE 788256	876287	220.10
20 11 –3	CREDIT NOTE 12218	876287	(22.01)
		CHEQUE TOTAL	698.09

preparing a cheque

When issuing the payment cheque you should complete in pen (not pencil):

- the correct date
- the name of the payee (person receiving the money)
- the amount in words
- the amount in figures (which should be the same as the amount in words)
- the counterfoil (date, amount, payee)

You will also need to obtain an authorised signature. No room should be left on the cheque for additions or alterations; any blank spaces should be ruled through with a single line. Any errors made should be corrected and an authorised signature placed next to the alteration.

Date *31/10/-3*

Pay
*Cool Socks
Limited*

£ *249.57*

238628

Albion Bank PLC
7 The Avenue
Broadfield BR1 2AJ

Date *31 October 20-3*

90 47 17

Pay *Cool Socks Limited*

Two hundred and forty nine pounds 57p

A/c payee only

£ *249.57 —*

TRENDS

V Williams

238628   90 47 17   11719512

the payment cheque

payment by BACS or Faster Payments

All BACS transfers or Faster Payments must be communicated to the supplier by means of a posted, faxed, or emailed remittance advice, otherwise the supplier will not know that payment has been made until the bank statement is received, and even then it may be difficult to identify the origin of the payment.

If the supplier does not know payment has been received, he or she may start chasing up the debt, which could prove embarrassing!

The bank details for the supplier receiving the payment will normally be set out on the bottom of the statement of account sent out by the supplier.

A BACS remittance advice is illustrated on the next page. Note the bank details (account number and sort code) at the bottom of the advice. Sometimes these details are abbreviated or even missed off altogther for security reasons.

```
BACS REMITTANCE ADVICE                    FROM: Trends
                                          4 Friar Street
                                          Broadfield BR1 3RF
TO
Cool Socks Limited
Unit 45 Elgar Estate, Broadfield, BR7 4ER    06 11 -3

Your ref        Our ref                                    Amount

787923          47609        BACS TRANSFER                  249.57


                                              TOTAL   249.57

THIS HAS BEEN PAID BY BACS CREDIT TRANSFER DIRECTLY INTO YOUR BANK ACCOUNT AT ALBION
BANK NO 11451226 SORT CODE 90 47 17
```

a remittance advice advising the sending of a BACS payment

PAYMENT BY BANK GIRO CREDIT

As explained in the last chapter (page 13), payment of bills has traditionally been made by **bank giro credit**, a paper-based bank payment transfer system. This is still used for bills such as gas, electricity, telephone and credit cards. It is slower and less efficient than electronic payment through the BACS or by Faster Payments and so is becoming less common.

This method involves the completion of a tear-off slip at the bottom of a bill – this is the **bank giro credit** – and the issue of a cheque for the appropriate amount. The bank giro credit and cheque are paid in at the bank and the money reaches the account being paid in three working days.

The internal procedures are much the same for any payment: the payment date has to be scheduled and the cheque issued and authorised.

CONTROL AND AUTHORISATION OF PAYMENTS

spending limits

In order to avoid fraud or unchecked spending within a business, all payments must be controlled and authorised. Incoming invoices must normally be stamped, and signed or initialled by an authorised person before being passed for payment. This is part of an overall system whereby no payment can be made without the necessary authority. The system will vary from business to business, but the following elements will usually be found:

- the larger the payment, the more senior the person who needs to authorise it; often each level of management has a money limit imposed – for example a new vehicle will need to be authorised by senior management
- when an item of expenditure is authorised, the person giving their authority will sign or initial and date the supporting document, eg an invoice, a cheque requisition form giving authority for issue of a cheque

cheque signatures

While a business will have an internal system of signing for and authorising expenditure, it will also have a written agreement with the bank – a bank mandate – which will set out who can sign cheques. A limited company may, for example, allow one director to sign cheques up to £5,000, but will require two to sign cheques in excess of £5,000.

STANDING ORDERS

A business that needs to make regular payments, eg loan repayments to a finance company, completes a written authority (a mandate – see below) instructing the bank the payments to make, to whom, and when. The bank then sets up the instructions on its computer, and the payments are made electronically using BACS or Faster Payments, on the due dates.

STANDING ORDER MANDATE

To _____National_____ Bank

Address __45 High Street, Hightown, HT1 7FG_____

PLEASE PAY TO

Bank __Western_____ Branch __Radstock_____ Sort code | 33 09 87 |

Beneficiary __Mendip Loan Brokers_____ Account number | 29384729 |

The sum of | £ 100.00 | Amount in words __one hundred pounds only_____

Date of first payment __1 April 20-3_____ Frequency of payment __1st monthly_____

Until __1 March 20-8_____ Reference __FTL294231_____

Account to be debited | Janus Limited | Account number | 22472434 |

SIGNATURE(S) ....*Archie Rice*...

If it is a business which is setting up the standing order, it is important that the mandate form is signed by a person (or persons) authorised to do so – it will often be the person(s) authorised to sign cheques and bank transfers.

BACS DIRECT CREDITS

Businesses often need to make **regular** payments of **variable** amounts, eg:

- paying wages on pay day
- making payments to established suppliers at the end of each month

The banks have established a BACS **direct credit** system to process these variable payments. Whenever the payments are due to be paid the business sends the bank a schedule (faxed or sent electronically) setting out the details of the payments.

setting up a direct credit system

To set up a direct credit system the bank needs written instructions from the customer before the amounts can be deducted from the account. The details needed by the bank are:

- the name of the 'beneficiary' – the business or person that is to receive the money, eg supplier, employee, insurance company, hire purchase company, etc
- the details of the beneficiary's bank:
  – bank branch and sort code number
  – bank account number
- a unique reference number for each beneficiary (eg a supplier account number or employee number) which is used each time payment is to be made

operating a direct credit system

At the end of each month, for example, the accounts department might draw up a list of the suppliers to be paid and a schedule of employees to be paid. These details will need checking and authorising before instructions are given to the bank. All the business has to do each time payment is to be made is to complete and send to the bank a schedule setting out the payment date, the people being paid, their reference number and the amount – an example is shown on the next page. The schedules may be sent to the bank by post, fax, telephone, or more commonly these days by online instructions. The bank will then process these details through its computers, and payments will be made automatically via the BACS system on the due date.

Case Study

PAYING SUPPLIERS BY DIRECT CREDIT

City Traders is a fashion shop based in Mereford. To help the business cut the costs of paying its suppliers the bank has suggested its Direct Credit system. City Traders has provided the suppliers' banking details (sort code and account number) together with an identifying payee reference number in advance for the bank to enter in its computer system. City Traders then writes the monthly payment details on the bank schedule shown below, which is faxed to the bank on Wednesday 24 September. The suppliers will be paid on Friday 26 September.

Mercian Bank PLC
Direct Credit Schedule

Bank branch... Mereford

Originator name. City Traders ..... reference.. 07246

Date .. 24/9/20-3

Branch	Account no	Name	Payee no	Amount
45-45-62	10386394	Trendsetters	234	250.00
56-67-23	22347342	FitMan Delivery Co	344	129.76
40-47-07	42472411	Jamesons Ltd	634	450.67
76-87-44	56944491	R Patel	123	409.79
33-00-77	23442413	R D Little Ltd	264	305.78
59-99-01	46244703	Mazzini Import Company	197	560.85
		PAYMENT TOTAL		2106.85

Please make the above payments to reach the payees on .... 26/9/20-3 .... (date)

Please debit account no...... 87620261 .... with the sum of £... 2106.85 ....

authorised signature...... *D.Craig* ....

BACS DIRECT DEBITS

The direct debit system is useful for businesses that receive a large number of variable payments, eg insurance companies and power utilities:

■ direct debits can be used for either fixed and variable amounts and/or where the time intervals between payments vary

■ it is the business receiving the money that prepares the computer instructions requesting the payer's bank account for payment through the banking system; a direct debit is like a standing order or direct credit operating backwards

paper-based direct debit instructions

The traditional procedure for setting up a direct debit is for the customer making payment to complete and sign a written authority (mandate) prepared by the beneficiary (the person getting the money, eg an insurance company); this is then returned to the beneficiary (eg the insurance company). The payment details are then posted off or sent electronically to the beneficiary's bank so that the computer instructions can be set up. The original form is then returned to the payer's bank. An example of a form is shown below.

<table>
<tr>
<td>
DIRECT Debit
</td>
<td colspan="2">
Tradesure Insurance Company
PO Box 134, Helliford, HL9 6TY

Originator's Identification Number 914208
</td>
</tr>
<tr>
<td colspan="3">
Reference (to be completed by Tradesure Insurance) .... 03924540234 ....

Please complete the details <u>and return this form to Tradesure Insurance</u>
</td>
</tr>
<tr>
<td colspan="2">
name and address of bank/building society

National Bank plc
Market Street
Netherway
MR7 9YT

account name

Grecian Travel Services
</td>
<td>
instructions to bank/building society

• I instruct you to pay direct debits from my account at the request of Tradesure Insurance Company.
• The amounts are variable and may be debited on various dates.
• I understand that Tradesure Insurance Company may change the amounts and dates after giving me prior notice.
• I will inform the bank/building society if I wish to cancel this instruction.
• I understand that if any direct debit is paid which breaks the terms of this instruction, the bank/building society will make a refund.
</td>
</tr>
<tr>
<td>
account number

10318736

sort code

76 54 29
</td>
<td>
signature(s)

M Callapolos
</td>
<td>
date

1 April 20-3
</td>
</tr>
</table>

a direct debit mandate form

AUDDIS and the paperless direct debit

Setting up a paper-based direct debit can be a protracted and expensive process, open to error and delay. As a consequence BACS now allows the direct debit payment details to be sent electronically by a system known as AUDDIS (Automated Direct Debit Instruction Service).

AUDDIS is used:

- by businesses such as insurance companies to send direct debit details (received in **writing** from customers) **electronically** to the customer's bank for validation - this system is therefore only partly 'paperless'

- to set up direct debit instructions from customers without using any paper instructions at all, eg the online completion of a direct debit mandate by a customer – this is the **paperless direct debit**

An example of the **paperless direct debit** is a customer wanting to set up a direct debit for an insurance policy on the insurance company's website. Using the AUDDIS system, the customer does not have to sign anything. The instructions (including bank account number, account name and bank sort code) are input by the customer online on the screen and passed electronically to the insurance company. The details are then sent electronically to the banking system – to the insurance company's bank for setting up and then to the customer's bank for approval and validation.

ELECTRONIC AND PAPER-BASED LARGER PAYMENTS

As explained in the last chapter, large payments may be made by both electronic and also by paper-based means.

CHAPS (Clearing House Automated Payments System) is used for high value **electronic** same-day payments sent by the banks through their computer networks. CHAPS is used, for example, by solicitors when they are arranging the purchase and sale of property for clients. It can also be used for any high value payment, either within the UK or internationally, in sterling or in currency. CHAPS payments cannot be cancelled after they have been sent.

Bank drafts, on the other hand are **paper-based** payments and can be posted or sent by courier. An organisation may have to make a large purchase – for example a new warehouse – and be asked to pay by bank draft. A bank draft is essentially a cheque written out by a bank and is as good as that bank in terms of certainty of payment. It is practically as secure as cash, but without the security risks that handling cash involves. A bank draft cannot be cancelled or stopped once it has been issued, but a forged bank draft is only worth the paper it is written on, ie nothing.

COMPANY CREDIT CARDS

Many businesses, including those that employ staff such as sales reps, often set up a company credit card scheme for paying expenses. This convenient and useful scheme allows company representatives to have credit cards for paying bills related to the company's business, eg rail tickets, accommodation and food. The credit card account is settled by the company which is then able to monitor the expenses incurred by its employees.

ONLINE BANKING

To save paper and expense banks encourage their customers to manage their accounts and payments online. Online banking allows customers:

- to get balances and view past transactions
- to download up-to-date statements
- to make payments from one account to another
- to set up standing orders

This makes day-to-day management of the finances of a business much simpler. The bank accounts can be monitored 24 hours a day, and greater control can be exercised over payments and receipts.

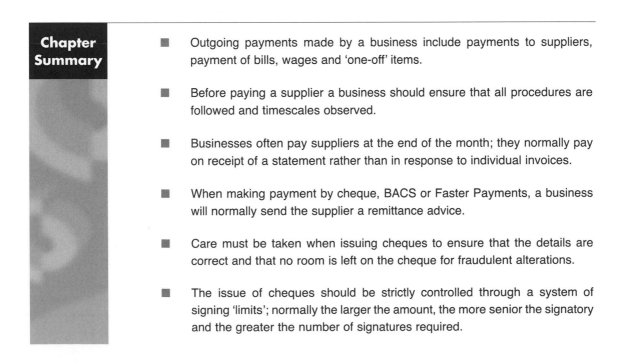

Chapter Summary

- Outgoing payments made by a business include payments to suppliers, payment of bills, wages and 'one-off' items.

- Before paying a supplier a business should ensure that all procedures are followed and timescales observed.

- Businesses often pay suppliers at the end of the month; they normally pay on receipt of a statement rather than in response to individual invoices.

- When making payment by cheque, BACS or Faster Payments, a business will normally send the supplier a remittance advice.

- Care must be taken when issuing cheques to ensure that the details are correct and that no room is left on the cheque for fraudulent alterations.

- The issue of cheques should be strictly controlled through a system of signing 'limits'; normally the larger the amount, the more senior the signatory and the greater the number of signatures required.

- Payments may be made through the inter-bank transfer system either in paper form or electronically through computer links.

- Bank giro credits, which take three working days to reach their destination account, are preprinted and are used for paying bills and settling credit card accounts.

- The majority of day-to-day bank computer-based payments are made through the BACS and Faster Payments. The BACS takes three working days to clear and the Faster Payments Service takes two hours.

- A standing order is authorised by the customer in writing and instructs the bank to make regular payments to the beneficiary. These are processed through the BACS or by Faster Payments.

- If a business needs to send a number of BACS payments on a regular basis but with differing amounts each time – eg when paying regular suppliers – it can authorise the bank to set up a BACS direct credit system. All it needs to do each month is to complete a bank schedule listing and authorising the amounts due and the accounts to which they have to be sent.

- A BACS direct debit is authorised by the customer in writing, over the telephone or the internet and instructs the bank to allow the beneficiary to take sums of money through the BACS from the customer's bank account.

- AUDDIS (Automated Direct Debit Instruction Service) allows direct debit customer instructions to be captured electronically (eg online) and sent to the paying and receiving banks without the need for any paper documentation.

- Another method of bank-to-bank computer payment is provided by CHAPS. These are computer inter-bank same-day guaranteed payments, usually for large amounts. They are used by solicitors for property purchases and businesses for large purchases.

- Other methods of payment used by businesses include:
  - company credit cards for use by employees for expenses
  - bank drafts (bank cheques which are 'as good as cash')

- The growth of internet banking has given businesses greater control and flexibility over making payments, and at the same time has allowed them to monitor their bank accounts more closely.

remittance advice	a document sent by the buyer to the supplier to provide details of the payment being made
bank giro credit	a paper slip which passes through the bank clearing system to the bank of the business receiving payment
BACS	the BACS system (Bankers Automated Clearing Services) passes payments through the banking system by computer transfer
Faster Payments	same-day value bank-to-bank payments service for smaller and medium-sized payments
standing order	a BACS transfer or Faster Payment where the person paying the money authorises a series of regular payments through his/her bank
BACS direct credit	a system whereby periodic and variable amount payments can be made through the BACS system, eg settling supplier accounts or paying wages; the payer completes a schedule setting out the amounts and beneficiaries and passes it to the bank for processing
BACS direct debit	regular and variable BACS payments, set up by the organisation receiving the payments and authorised by the person making the payments
AUDDIS	AUDDIS (Automated Direct Debit Instruction Service) allows the customer to authorise a direct debit by telephone or online and the beneficiary to send those instructions electronically to the payer's bank
CHAPS	a CHAPS payment (CHAPS = Clearing House Automated Payments System) is a high-value same-day inter-bank computer payment
company credit card	a credit card – in the name of the company – issued to a company employee and used for paying expenses
bank draft	a cheque written out by a bank and purchased by a customer as a payment which is 'as good as cash'

Activities

2.1 The BACS remittance advice is normally attached to the cheque sent in settlement of an account. True or false?

2.2 Why do you think a cheque should not be completed in pencil?

2.3 Explain why a limited company business has to sign a bank mandate.

2.4 (a) What is the difference between a standing order and a direct debit?

State whether a standing order or a direct debit is the better method for the following payments, and why:

(b) a repayment of a fixed loan: £125 per month for five years

(c) a monthly insurance premium which is likely to increase over the years.

2.5 Name two commonly-used methods suitable for making high value 'one-off' payments:

(a) a paper-based payment

(b) a computer-based payment

2.6 Company credit cards are a popular means of making payment.

(a) State one advantage to the employee of the company credit card.

(b) State one advantage to the employer of the company credit card.

For the remainder of the Activities in this chapter you are to assume the role of an assistant in the Accounts Department of Nimrod Drainage Limited (a VAT-registered company). Part of your day's work is the preparation of remittance advices and cheques for payments to suppliers. You are not required to sign the cheques. The date is 30 April 20-3.

2.7 Your line manager, Ivor Cash, hands you on 30 April a list of authorised invoices from Jaeger Building Supplies which you are to pay. The monthly payment date is always the last working day of the month. Calculate the amount of the cheque you will have to make out to send with the remittance advice. You do not need to complete any documents.

invoice date	payment terms	invoice total (£)
31 March	30 days	125.89
2 April	30 days	14,658.95
3 April	2.5% cash discount for settlement within 7 days	345.50
9 April	30 days	125.00

2.8 Your line manager hands you a statement from Mercia Wholesalers, Unit 12 Riverside Industrial Park, Mereford MR2 7GH, with a note, indicating the following invoices to be paid, and a credit note to be set off against payment:

Invoice 8765 dated 12 March 20-3, your order number 5517, £765.25

Invoice 8823 dated 2 April 20-3, your order number 5792, £3,567.80

Credit note CN 3420 dated 25 April 20-3 (your ref R/N 5168), £250.00

Complete the remittance advice and cheque set out below. Note that the total of the credit note should be shown in the money column in brackets, indicating that it is a deduction from the payment.

TO			REMITTANCE ADVICE
			FROM
			Nimrod Drainage
			Unit 6, Riverside Park
			Mereford
			MR4 5TF
Cheque no.		**Date**	Tel 01908 761200 Fax 01908 761900 VAT REG GB 0745 8383 46
date	**your reference**	**our reference**	**payment amount**
		CHEQUE TOTAL	

National Bank PLC
Mereford Branch
10 Cathedral Street, Mereford, MR1 5DE

Date _____

35 09 75

Date _____

Pay _____ only

A/c payee only

£ ____ —

NIMROD DRAINAGE LIMITED
Director   Director

£ _____

000451   000451   35 09 75   12034875

2.9 As an accounts assistant at Nimrod Drainage Limited you have to process the documentation for a wide variety of payments to employees, suppliers and for other business expenses such as one-off purchases, travel costs and bills.

What method of payment would you <u>normally</u> expect to use for the following:

(a) paying wages to employees who have a bank account

(b) paying the electricity bill which is sent to the business every three months

(c) buying a new Porsche car for the Managing Director

(d) paying travelling expenses for sales representatives

(e) sending £800,000 to a firm of solicitors for the purchase of new premises

2.10 The date is 30 April 20-3. Your supervisor, Ivor Cash, hands you two documents (shown on the next two pages):

• a blank standing order form provided by the bank

• a direct debit instruction received from Tradesure Insurance Company

Ivor is in rather a rush and asks you to process the two documents, and to return them to the appropriate address with a compliments slip. He also leaves you a piece of paper with written instructions:

Note from: Ivor   30 April 20-3

Hire Purchase Payments

12 monthly instalments of £350 to Broadbent Finance from 15 May 20-3, under reference BE/6637.

Bank details Barclays, Eveshore, 30 98 15, Account 72627161.
Debit our Account 12034875

You are to:

(a) complete the forms as required (look at the Nimrod Drainage cheque on the previous page for the banking details such as the sort code and account number)

(b) state to which address you will send them

(c) describe any other procedure which you may have to carry out before sending off the forms

Note that as an accounts assistant you are not authorised to sign cheques or other payment instructions.

STANDING ORDER MANDATE

To _____ Bank

Address _____

PLEASE PAY TO

Bank _____   Branch _____   Sort code [   ]

Beneficiary   Account number [   ]

The sum of [£   ]   Amount in words _____

Date of first payment _____   Frequency of payment _____

Until _____   Reference _____

Account to be debited [   ]   Account number [   ]

SIGNATURE(S)   ....

                       .... date...........................

DIRECT Debit

Tradesure Insurance Company

PO Box 134, Helliford, HL9 6TY

Originator's Identification Number 914208

Reference (to be completed by Tradesure Insurance) .... 03924540234 ....

Please complete the details <u>and return this form to Tradesure Insurance</u>

name and address of bank/building society

----

account name

instructions to bank/building society

- I instruct you to pay direct debits from my account at the request of Tradesure Insurance Company.
- The amounts are variable and may be debited on various dates.
- I understand that Tradesure Insurance Company may change the amounts and dates after giving me prior notice.
- I will inform the bank/building society if I wish to cancel this instruction.
- I understand that if any direct debit is paid which breaks the terms of this instruction, the bank/building society will make a refund.

account number

sort code

signature(s)

date

3 Receiving and recording payments

this chapter covers...

The last chapter described the different ways of paying using the banking system. This chapter concentrates on the practicalities of the payments system. It explains the different ways in which money paid by customers is received by a business:

- *cash*

- *cheques*

- *BACS transfers and Faster Payments*

In each case it describes the checks that should be made and the security procedures carried out to ensure that:

■ *the right amount is received*

■ *from the right person or business*

■ *the payment is properly authorised and will not be refused by the bank*

This chapter sets out the procedures that should be followed by the business in documenting and recording those payments, for example:

■ *checking cash received and issuing receipts*

■ *checking cheques received*

■ *receiving and processing incoming payments by debit card and credit card*

■ *recording incoming payments on remittance lists, cash books and cash tills*

The next chapter explains how money is paid into the bank and is then recorded by the bank on the bank statement.

INCOMING PAYMENTS

Payments can be received by a business in a variety of ways:

- cash (ie banknotes and coins)
- cheques
- credit card and debit card transactions (which can be manually or electronically processed)
- electronic inter-bank transfer: BACS, Faster Payments, CHAPS

The current trend is for more and more payments to be made electronically, although low value payments are still frequently made by cash.

CASH

Cash, as noted above, is commonly used for most low value transactions, and we still have not reached the 'cashless society' which is sometimes talked about. Devices such as **tap and go** debit cards, which do not require a PIN number are becoming increasingly popular and widely used for small purchases.

Nowadays, however, as far as the business accepting payments in cash is concerned, the main disadvantage of cash is the security problem (avoiding theft), and the risk of receiving forged notes.

receiving payment in cash

For a business receiving sums of money in the form of cash it is necessary for an employee to count the cash received and check it against the amount handed over.

Change will need to be given when the exact amount is not paid. For example if someone buys a magazine for £5.99 and hands over a £10 note:

Sale of magazine	£5.99
Amount given by customer	£10.00
Change to be given by shop	£4.01

The amount of change is the difference between the amount handed over and the amount of the sale. A till will normally indicate the amount of change to be given after the amount handed over has been entered through the keypad.

Often when payment is made in cash, a receipt is given: this can take the form of a till receipt, such as is given in a shop, or, less commonly, a handwritten receipt. Look at these two examples of receipts:

Everest Sports	←	retailer
15 High St Mereford	←	address
08 10 20-3 15.07	←	date and time of transaction
Salesperson Tina	←	salesperson
Tennis balls 5.99	←	goods purchased
Shin guards 18.99	←	goods purchased
TOTAL 24.98	←	total due
CASH 40.00	←	£40 (probably two £20 notes) given by the customer
CHANGE 15.02	←	change given
Thank you for your custom	←	personal message to help public relations
Please retain this receipt in case of any query	←	advice to retain receipt in case of a problem with the goods
VAT REG 373 2888 11	←	VAT Registration number of retailer

a till receipt

ENIGMA MUSIC LIMITED   *receipt*   **958**

13 High Street, Mereford MR1 2TF
VAT Reg 343 7645 23

Customer ....*R V Williams*..........date ...*3 Oct 20-3*...

'Golden Oldies' by J Moore	£20.00
	£20.00
VAT @ 20%	£4.00
Total	£24.00

a hand-written receipt

tills and cash floats

At the end of the day it is necessary to 'cash up' by totalling the cash held and then agreeing that total with the amount that the till started with at the beginning of the day, plus what has been received during the day. Most cash tills start each day with a float of cash and so the amount in the till at the end of the day should be:

cash float at start

plus cash from sales made during the day (listed on the till roll)

equals amount of cash held at end of day

A cash float will be kept back for the following day, and any surplus will be transferred to the safe for paying into the bank next day.

guidelines for cash handling

Cash is often a target for theft – and regrettably not only from people outside the business. General security guidelines for looking after cash received will vary according to the size and type of business:

- cash should be kept in a cash till or in a cash box which should be kept locked when not in use
- the keys should be retained under the control of the cashier
- as little cash as is practically possible should be kept in tills
- cash should be paid into the bank as soon as possible

'topping up' the petty cash

The business may also operate a petty cash system for making small payments. The cash will be kept in a locked metal box and will need to be 'topped up' from time-to-time to what is known as the **imprest amount** to bring it up to a fixed level. The principle is basically the same as filling up a car with fuel – you put back in the same amount you have used. Care will have to be taken when transferring money from the main cash fund to the petty cash box: security precautions should be observed.

ACCEPTING CHEQUES

Businesses receive cheques as a form of payment in a variety of ways, normally through the post with a remittance advice, or directly over the counter, as in the case of a shop (although this is becoming far less common).

Before a cheque is paid into the bank it is very important that it is checked to make sure that it is technically correct.

If you are receiving payment by cheque, whether it is direct from the customer over the counter or through the post on a remittance advice, there are a number of basic checks to carry out:

- is the cheque signed? – it is invalid if it is not
- is the payee's name correct? – it should be changed and initialled by the drawer (person writing out the cheque) if it is not
- is the cheque in date? – a cheque becomes out of date ('stale') and invalid after six months; note that if the date is missing, it may be written in
- do the words and figures agree? – the cheque may be returned by the bank if they do not

Study the cheque on the next page. The cheque was received by the payee on 21 October 2013. It is now 23 October. Is the cheque technically correct?

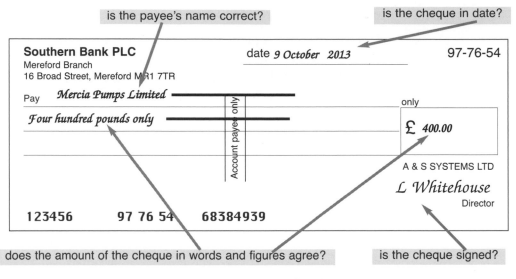

checking the cheque

The answer to 'is this cheque correct' is 'yes' – as long as the payee's name is 'Mercia Pumps Limited'.

But if the business accepting payment by cheque is inefficient and does not carry out the checks listed on the previous page, the cheque concerned may be returned to the business's bank after it has been paid in, and the amount of the cheque deducted from the business's bank account. This is known as a **dishonoured cheque**.

DISHONOURED CHEQUES

returned cheques

A business may be in the unfortunate position of having paid in a cheque and then discovering that the cheque has been returned to its bank **unpaid**, and the amount of the cheque then deducted from the business' bank account.

The bank will normally post the cheque back to the business that paid it in. If this happens to you when you are working in an Accounts Department and you receive a returned (dishonoured) cheque, you will see that it will have one of a number of reasons for return written or stamped across the top:

■ **refer to drawer** – the person or business that has written out the cheque (the issuer or 'drawer') has no money in the bank; this is bad news for you and you will have to contact him or her for an explanation!

This answer is often abbreviated to 'RD'

- **refer to drawer, please represent** – this means that there was not enough money in the account to meet the cheque, but that the cheque has been sent through the clearing again (represented) in the hope that it will be paid when it reaches the issuers bank the second time (note that in this case the cheque will *not* be sent back to the payee)

  This answer is abbreviated to 'RDPR'

- **payment countermanded by order of drawer** – the cheque has been **stopped** – in other words the issuer (drawer) has told the bank that the cheque should not be paid, maybe because of some dispute or a cancelled order; you should contact the issuer to find out the reason

- **technical problems** – as mentioned before, payment of a cheque may be refused by the bank for technical reasons; you may get a cheque sent back to you with a reason written on the cheque such such as 'signature required', 'words and figures differ' and 'out of date'

  This means that you will have to contact the issuer of the cheque (drawer) for a signature (if it is missing), or an alteration (which will have to be signed by the drawer) if the returned cheque is out of date. As you will appreciate, this reinforces the point that a cheque must be carefully checked when it is received in payment.

ACCEPTING CARD PAYMENTS

By far the most common method of processing a debit or credit card payment for a customer who calls in person is **'chip and PIN'** – here the customer authorises payment on a terminal using a four digit number known as a 'PIN' (Personal Identification Number).

terminal 'chip and PIN' sales – customer present

This method of accepting payment by credit and debit cards involves the cardholder's card being inserted in a card reader device with a keypad, eg in a supermarket or a restaurant. The keypad may be wired into a till (as in a supermarket) or it may be remote and mobile, operating through a bluetooth system (as in a restaurant). The customer then confirms the sales transaction (or the bill for the meal) by keying in a four digit number (PIN) which should only be known to the cardholder. If there is any problem (eg the card is stolen or the limit exceeded) authorisation will be refused. This form of payment is good for the seller because it is fully guaranteed.

Mobile card readers are also available for businesses such as taxis and market stall traders.

'Chip and PIN' was introduced for three main reasons:

- it greatly increases the efficiency of checkouts because it saves time
- it cuts down on card fraud because it is a far more secure method of making payment
- it removes the need for telephone calls to be made for authorisation for transactions over the 'floor limit' of the seller (the 'floor limit' is the amount over which a telephone request for authorisation had to be made)

Major benefits of the system are that a chip and PIN transaction avoids the retailer having to carry out all the security checks needed when a signature is required, and the payment is then guaranteed. There are, of course, some common sense precautions which should be taken by the retailer, for example making sure that other customers (or employees) cannot watch or somehow record the PIN being entered.

mail order/telephone sales – customer not present

Buying goods and services by credit card and debit card over the telephone, and by mail order is also very common. Obviously 'chip and PIN' cannot be used for this because the customer is not present. Most businesses will therefore use an electronic '**customer not present**' terminal which will be linked to the card merchant electronically. Note that a very small minority of businesses may still use a mechanical imprinter.

When accepting '**customer not present**' payment by debit or credit card by telephone or mail order, the following details must be obtained:

- the card number, the three digit security code, and expiry date
- the issue number and/or start date of any debit card
- the name and initials of the cardholder as shown on the card
- the cardholder's card statement address
- the cardholder's signature (mail order only)

One important difference for mail order, telephone and internet sales is that payment is not necessarily guaranteed. The **chargeback** system means that a purchaser who places an order and then receives faulty or incorrect goods can claim the money back from the card issuing company who refunds it to the purchaser's account. The money is then 'charged back' to the seller. Chargeback can also be used if an unauthorised fraudulent purchase has been made by someone other than the cardholder.

internet sales – customer not present

Businesses which have online facilities for selling their products from their websites carry out these sales on a 'remote control' basis. They obviously do not deal with these customers personally. The customers order and pay for the goods online using a credit or debit card and all the business has to do is despatch the goods (eg an online shop) or provide the service (eg a flight or hotel booking). The money is credited (added) directly to the bank account of the business by the card merchant that processes the payment.

When purchasing online the customer will have to provide many of the card details also required for mail order and telephone sales, for example:

■ the customer's name

■ card address and any delivery address if it is different

■ card details: card number, expiry date, security code

■ the issue number and/or start date of any debit card

Some internet sites will 'store' card and address details for customers so when making further purchases the customer is saved the bother of re-entering all the details. This 'saving' of data raises the question of online security and dangers of fraud and identity theft. Businesses setting up online selling facilities have to ensure that the security of the system is as safe as it can be by using software which encrypts (encodes) the data so that payment details – including card numbers and security codes – remain secret. The padlock symbol on a website means that the data is encrypted.

The mechanics of how the payment from an internet purchase reaches the bank account of the seller is explained in detail on page 68. The business will receive from the card merchant a schedule of the payments received which it can check against its bank statement.

CARD PAYMENTS – OLD-FASHIONED METHODS

important note

This section deals with methods of dealing with card payments which are now rarely seen. They do, however, still exist and are covered by the AAT Standards. When studying and revising this topic you are advised to concentrate on the methods already covered on the last three pages.

'customer present' sales requiring a signature

This older method of using a terminal to process card payments is rapidly being superseded by 'chip and PIN' (see page 47). It may occasionally be used, for example, when the 'chip and PIN' system has broken down. With this 'signature' system the assistant operating the terminal should:

■ in the case of a shop till, 'swipe' the card through the card reader – this 'captures' the details encoded in the magnetic stripe on the reverse of the card or in the chip embedded in the card

- the card merchant's system checks automatically that the card number is valid, the card has not been lost or stolen and there is enough money (or limit) available to pay for the transaction

- if all is well, each transaction will be allowed to pass through; if it is not, the customer will be asked to pay another way

- if the amount is above the 'floor limit', a telephone call to the card merchant will be required to authorise the transaction

- the till prints a two-part receipt which includes space for the cardholder's signature

- the customer signs, and the signature is compared with that on the card

- the customer is handed the top-copy of the receipt, and the other copy is kept in the event of a query in the future

There are a number of **checks** that should be made on the rare occasions when accepting payment authorised by a signature – eg if the 'chip and PIN' system has gone offline and a signature will be needed. These checks apply equally to debit cards and to credit cards. You should make sure that:

- the card has an appropriate logo, eg 'Maestro'

- the card has a magnetic stripe on the reverse or an embedded chip

- the card has not expired

- the signature on the card is consistent and has not been tampered with, and the card has not been defaced or mutilated in any way

mechanical 'push-pull' imprinter machine

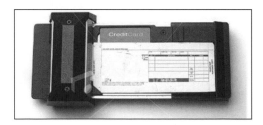

This rather ancient system is now rarely used, but it is still valid and can occasionally be found. The procedure is:

- check that the card has not expired and place it on the imprinter

- imprint the sales voucher by hand on the 'push-pull' mechanical printer (see picture on left) – if you look at a debit or credit card you will see that card number, name and start and expiry dates are embossed to enable them to be imprinted on the voucher

- complete the sales voucher with date, details of goods, and the amount

- the customer signs the imprinted sales voucher, and the signature should be compared with that on the card

- if the payment is above a certain amount – the **floor limit** (which varies according to the type of business) it will be necessary to telephone the card merchant company to obtain an authorisation code for the transaction – the authorisation code is recorded on the sales voucher

- the top copy of the sales voucher is handed to the customer, and the other three copies are retained

- of the three copies of the sales voucher which are retained, the white copy is treated in the same way as a cheque, and is kept in the till and added to the cheques and cash received to give the total sales figure; the other two copies (yellow and blue) are kept in the event of a query in the future

- the white copy of the sales voucher kept in the till is then banked along with the cash and cheques (see next chapter)

CHECKING PAYMENTS AGAINST DOCUMENTATION

It is important that incoming payments received from customers are checked against any documentation that the supplier receives. This is to ensure that the correct amount is received and that no future disputes can arise – for example "We sent you £450, that's what it says on our advice" ... "No you didn't, you only sent us £405, that's what it shows on your account."

The most common type of document which advises the amount of a payment is the **remittance advice**. Payments from customers can be received either through the post, or through the bank as inter-bank transfers. A remittance advice will be issued in both instances by the person paying (see next page).

cheque payments – remittance advice

Any cheque received through the post should be checked for technical irregularities and also against the remittance advice. The business receiving payment must check that the total of the items being paid less any credit due equals the amount of the cheque. Failure to carry out this simple check could cause problems later on if there is a discrepancy. Any discrepancies should be queried with the customer without delay.

inter-bank transfers – BACS remittance advice

An increasing number of payments are now made automatically from bank account to bank account, normally on the instructions of the payer, through the BACS system or the Faster Payments Service. Because no cheque is issued, payment is made more quickly and more cheaply. With this system the buyer sends to the seller an electronic remitance advice. The business receiving payment will have to check each advice carefully against the bank statement when it arrives to ensure that the correct amount has been received.

Two remittance advices are illustrated in the last chapter – a cheque advice (page 26) and and a BACS advice (page 28).

RECORDING MONEY RECEIVED

The individual amounts of money received should be recorded by the business. The way in which they are recorded will depend on the way in which they are received. The fact that the amounts are recorded will help security by discouraging theft by employees.

cash tills

Money received over a counter is likely to be recorded on a cash till tally roll or electronic till memory – the totals on the till roll or memory can then be checked with the actual money received, ready for paying into the bank. The security of cash tills is tightly controlled: they are operated by a security key and any transfer of change is recorded.

remittance lists (postal items)

Cheques and other money received may be recorded manually on a **remittance list**. 'Remittance list' just means a list of what you have been sent. It can record items received through the post by a business, or it can be used at the counter of old-fashioned shops instead of a cash till. A remittance list for items received through the post is likely to include columns for the date, sender, the nature of the 'remittance' amount, and, as a security measure, the signature of the person opening the post. A remittance list will normally be totalled from time-to-time.

date	sender	remittance	amount	signature
12.3.20-3	Travers Toys Ltd	cheque	234.50	G Palmer
12.3.20-3	Grampian Traders	bank draft	10,500.00	G Palmer
12.3.20-3	Mrs D Dodds	cash	14.50	R Patel
12.3.20-3	Mercia Foods	cheque	450.00	G Palmer

extract from a remittance list for items received through the post

cash book – a book of prime entry

The cash book is the book of prime entry for money amounts received and paid out by the organisation in the form of cash and as items passed through the bank account. All the receipts referred to in this chapter will eventually pass through the cash book.

■ **Incoming payments** can be received in a number of ways: cash, cheque, credit and debit card, electronic transfers and internet sales.

■ **Receipts** are often issued for cash payments; either till receipts or handwritten receipts.

■ **Cash** in a till will be counted up at the end of each day; the amount should equal the takings for the day plus any 'float' held in the till.

■ **Cheques** should be examined carefully when received as payment, details to be checked include the signature, payee's name, the date and the amount in words and figures.

■ Cheques returned by the bank unpaid are known as **dishonoured cheques** – this can happen if the cheque has technical errors, or is stopped, or if the person or business issuing it does not have the money in the bank.

■ **Debit cards** are commonly accepted as a means of payment in place of cash or cheques. They are normally processed using a 'chip and PIN' electronic terminal.

■ Payment can also be accepted by **credit card** – normally using a 'chip and PIN' electronic terminal.

■ If a business uses a 'chip and PIN' electronic terminal or remote 'customer not present' terminal the money will be transferred electronically from the customer's bank account or credit card account to the business bank account.

■ Older methods of processing credit and debit card payments include the '**customer signature**' system using sales vouchers and also the antiquated '**imprinter**' machine. These methods are rapidly dying out.

■ Sales transactions over the **internet** are processed under secure conditions and the money transferred automatically to the seller's bank account.

■ When payments are accompanied by documentation such as a **remittance advice**, the payment should be checked against the documentation. Payment in this case is likely to be by cheque or by inter-bank transfer.

■ When money is received it should be **recorded**, both for security purposes and also as part of the operation of the accounting system. Forms of recording include the cash till roll, remittance lists and the cash book.

cash float	the amount of cash kept in a till at the end of the day to provide change when the till is next used
drawer of a cheque	the person who signs the bottom of the cheque – the customer from whose account the money is to be deducted
payee of a cheque	the person to whom the cheque is payable – normally specified on the first line of the cheque after the word 'pay'
dishonoured cheque	a cheque which is paid in but then returned unpaid to the payee because of a technical error or because the drawer does not have the money
debit card	a plastic card which enables customers to make payment for purchases without having to write out a cheque – payment is made electronically from the bank account
credit card	a plastic card issued by a credit card company which enables customers to make purchases and pay for them at a later date
chip and PIN	the technology for accepting payments by debit and credit cards where the customer enters a four digit number (PIN) into an electronic terminal
BACS	BACS stands for Bankers Automated Clearing Services, a body (owned by the banks) which organises computer payments between bank accounts
Faster Payments	a same day payment system (usually 2 hours) – the instructions are normally given by telephone or online or on a standing order
remittance advice	a document sent to the recipient of a payment, advising that a payment is being made
remittance list	a record of money amounts received by a business

Activities

3.1 You operate the cash till at the firm where you work. The following are the sales for one day:

		Amount of sale £	Notes and/or coin tendered
Customer	1	8.50	£10 note
	2	3.30	£10 note
	3	2.51	£5 note
	4	1.79	£5 note
	5	0.34	£1 coin
	6	6.22	£10 note
	7	12.76	£20 note
	8	1.42	two £1 coins
	9	6.54	£10 note
	10	3.08	£5 note

Calculate:

(a) the amount of change to be given to each customer

(b) the notes and/or coins that will be given in change, using the minimum number possible

3.2 If the cash till in Activity 3.1 had a float of £28.71 at the start of the day, how much cash should be held in the till after the sales from activity 1 had been made? Present your answer in the following form:

	£
cash float at start of day	28.71
plus sales made during the day	
equals amount of cash held at end of day	

3.3 You work as a shop counter assistant at New Era Lighting. You make a number of sales during the day (use today's date) which require the completion of a handwritten receipt. Complete the receipts set out on the next page. Include VAT on all purchases at 20%. All prices quoted here are catalogue prices and exclude VAT.

(a) 2 flexilamps @ £13.99, 2
60w light bulbs @ 85p, to
Mr George Ohm

NEW ERA LIGHTING 977

17 High Street, Mereford, MR1 2TF
VAT Reg 141 7654 23

CASH RECEIPT

Customer ....date..................

VAT	
TOTAL	

(b) 1 standard lamp @ £149.95,
1 13amp plug @ 99p, to Mr
Alex Bell

NEW ERA LIGHTING 978

17 High Street, Mereford, MR1 2TF
VAT Reg 141 7654 23

CASH RECEIPT

Customer ....date..................

VAT	
TOTAL	

(c) 2 external Georgian lamps
@ £35.99, to Tom Edison

NEW ERA LIGHTING 979

17 High Street, Mereford, MR1 2TF
VAT Reg 141 7654 23

CASH RECEIPT

Customer ....date..................

VAT	
TOTAL	

3.4 You work as an accounts assistant at Electron Games Limited. You have received the three cheques shown below though the post in settlement of customer accounts. Check them carefully and state what is wrong with them. Assume that the date today is 12 October 2013.

(a)

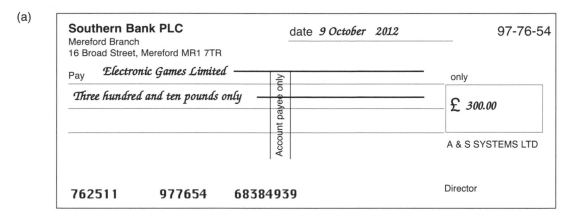

(b)

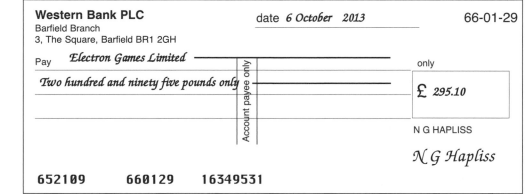

(c)

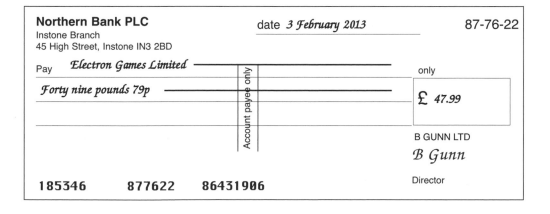

3.5 When making an online purchase with a credit card, the purchaser provides the following details onscreen:

	✔
account number, card number, security code	
card number, expiry date, security code	
account number, card number, expiry date	

Which one of these options is correct?

3.6 A business receives a remittance advice (shown below) which is unfortunately incomplete.

REMITTANCE ADVICE

TO

Bromyard Road Traders
187 Bromyard Road
Hereford
HF4 7BP

2 December 20-3

FROM

Helford Ltd
16 Kent Road
Manorfield
MA2 6GP

date	your reference	our reference	payment amount
04 11 -3	INVOICE 1896	8713	850.00
16 11 -3	INVOICE 1903	8920	450.50
23 11 -3	CREDIT NOTE 756	8920	(45.05)
		CHEQUE TOTAL	

(a) What should the total figure be?

(b) What form of payment will be used to settle the account in this case?

(c) What other two methods using electronic transfer of funds could be used?

3.7   If a cheque is returned to the business which has paid it in marked 'refer to drawer' it means that:

(a)   there is a technical problem with the cheque, for example it could be out of date

(b)   the issuer's signature is missing and will have to be obtained as soon as possible

(c)   the issuer of the cheque does not have enough money in the account to pay the cheque

(d)   the cashier must check the list of stolen cheques kept in the till drawer

Which one of these options is correct?

3.8   If a debit or credit card is used for making payment at a supermarket till using 'chip and PIN' the customer should:

(a)   enter the PIN number on the card reader and sign a voucher to authorise the payment

(b)   enter the PIN number on the card reader and tell the cashier the security number on the back of the card

(c)   enter the PIN number on the card reader and tell the cashier the PIN number to confirm the transaction

(d)   enter the PIN number on the card reader, making sure that no-one has seen them keying in the numbers

Which one of these options is correct?

3.9   When a mail order company accepts debit and credit card payments from customers who order goods through the post:

(a)   the payment to the seller will be guaranteed in all circumstances

(b)   the payment may not be guaranteed and may be refunded to the customer through 'chargeback'

(c)   the PIN number will need to be input on the mail order company's terminal

(d)   the PIN number and the three digit security code will need to be input on the terminal

Which one of these options is correct?

3.10   What is the purpose of 'encryption' of credit and debit card data in online payment processing? How can you tell from a website that data will be encrypted?

3.11   What is the difference between a remittance advice and a remittance list?

4 Paying into the bank

this chapter covers...

The last chapter dealt with the day-to-day detail of a business receiving payments in the form of cash, cheques, and debit and credit card transactions. It described the checks and precautions that have to be made to ensure that each transaction is secure and accurately recorded.

This chapter deals with the next step in the process and sets out the procedures for paying money into the bank and tracking incoming receipts made electronically.

Before reading this chapter you should be familiar with the contents of Chapter 1 'Banks, Building Societies and payment systems' (pages 2-19) which provides essential background information for dealing with building societies, banks and payment transactions.

This chapter specifically covers the areas of:

■ *how to prepare a paying-in slip for paying cash and cheques into the bank*

■ *checking the cash and cheques being paid in*

■ *preparing the credit card vouchers summary for paying in at the bank*

■ *paying in procedures*

■ *the need to pay in promptly, and security procedures for looking after money*

■ *automated payments into the bank account, online payments received and the need for security of electronic data*

■ *the format and content of a bank statement*

PAYING-IN SLIPS

Bank customers are issued with a book of **paying-in slips** (bank giro credits). These books are pre-printed and encoded with the customer's name and account number together with details of the bank branch. The details to be completed before paying in at the bank are:

■ a summary of the different categories of notes or coins being paid in, the amount of each category being entered on the slip

■ amounts and details of cheques being paid in, usually entered on the reverse of the slip, with the total entered on the front

■ the cash and cheques being paid in are totalled to give the amount being paid in

■ the counterfoil (the section on the left-hand side) is completed

■ the person paying in will sign the slip

A completed paying-in slip (both front and back) is illustrated below:

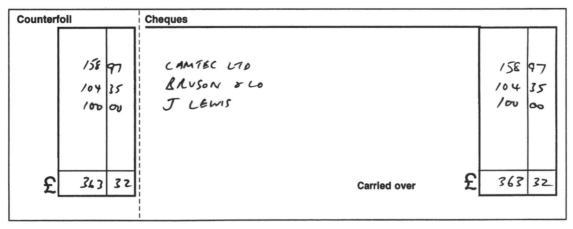

PROCEDURES FOR PAYING IN

the accounting process

Cash and cheques paid in at the bank will normally have been received by the business both as cash sales and also on remittance advices from customers. They are then entered in the cash book (a book of prime entry) as part of the accounting process.

preparing the cash

Bank notes should be counted, checked and sorted so that they all face the same way, but should be kept separate. Defaced (damaged) notes, and notes from Scotland and Northern Ireland are normally accepted by banks. Coins should be sorted into denominations, eg £2, £1, 50p and so on, and placed in the appropriate plastic money bags.

preparing the cheques

The cheques must first be examined carefully for any irregularities, such as:

- **signatures** – has the issuer signed the cheque?

- **payee** – if the name on the payee line is not the same as the name of the account into which it is being paid, the cheque will not be accepted by the bank

- **date** – is it out of date (over six months old)? is it post-dated (ie does it have a future date)? – if so, it cannot be paid in (but note that you can fill in a missing date and pay in the cheque)

- **words and figures** – are the money amounts the same?

The details of the cheques – the amounts and the customer names – may then be listed on the back of the paying-in slip, as in the illustration on the previous page.

If the number of cheques paid in is very large, there will not be room on the paying-in slip, so the cheque details may be listed on a separate schedule. Some banks accept instead a calculator tally-roll listing the amounts, the number of cheques, and the total money amount transferred to the front of the paying-in slip.

The important point is that the business paying in the cheques must keep a record of the cheque details in case of future queries, and in the unfortunate event of any of the cheques being 'dishonoured' – ie being returned unpaid.

reconciliation with the financial records

It is important that the paying-in slips are reconciled with the relevant financial and accounting records before the slips are taken to the bank. For example, the total of the paying-in slip could be agreed with the receipts shown in the cash book. Further reconciliations could be carried out between the cheque total and the remittance list and the cash total with the total taken from the cash tills. These reconciliations will highlight any errors – either in the records or on the paying-in slip.

paying in at the bank

At the bank the completed paying-in book is handed to the bank cashier together with the notes, coins, and cheques. The cashier counts the cash, ticks off the cheques and, if everything is correct, receipt stamps and initials the paying-in slip and counterfoil. The slip is retained by the bank for the amount to be credited to the account-holder, while the paying-in book is handed back, complete with the stamped up counterfoil. A business paying-in book is sometimes larger than the paying-in slip illustrated, and there may be a carbon copy which acts as a counterfoil.

security measures for cash handling – night safes

Care must be taken when taking large amounts of cash to the bank. If possible two staff members should visit the bank. If the amount is very large, for instance the takings from a department store, a security firm may be employed to carry the cash. If the cash is received by a business over the weekend or, late in the day, it may be placed in a special wallet and lodged in the bank's **night safe** – a small lockable door leading to a safe in the wall of the bank.

When a business pays in money to the bank, it will record the amount in its own records, the cash book.

CARD VOUCHER CLEARING – CARD MERCHANT SERVICES

As we saw in the last chapter, a sales voucher is the basic document which may be produced when a debit card and a credit card transaction are processed manually, although this is now very rare. The sales voucher may be produced as a result of an 'over-the-counter' sale or from a mail order or telephone sale. The details recorded on it will enable the card company to charge the amount to their customer's bank account (debit card transaction) or credit card account. The voucher, like a cheque, is paid in at the bank and sent to the card company and 'cleared'.

Although there are a number of different card companies – Mastercard and Visa for example – the normal practice is for the business accepting payment to sign an agreement with a separate company – the card merchant – which will accept all vouchers from cards issued by different companies. For example, a customer of The Royal Bank of Scotland (RBS) may sign an agreement with a company called Streamline (owned by The Royal Bank of Scotland) and accept payment by Mastercard and Visa and other cards.

The customer will pay in all credit card vouchers on the one paying-in slip and schedule (see below) at the The Royal Bank of Scotland or NatWest (owned by The Royal Bank of Scotland). The bank will pass them to Streamline, which will then process them by sending them to the issuing card company (Mastercard or Visa, for example). Streamline is only one of a number of 'card merchant' companies which will process credit card sales vouchers.

preparing card sales vouchers for paying in

The vouchers are paid in after completion of a three-part Retailer Summary, illustrated below and on the next page. In this case three sales vouchers are listed on the back of the summary.

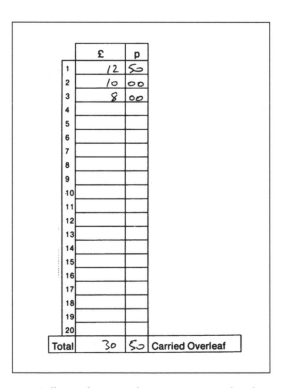

retailer sales voucher summary – back

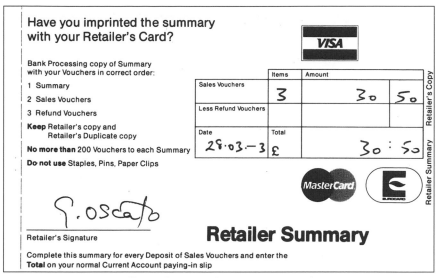

retailer sales voucher summary – front

The procedure for listing credit card sales vouchers on the retailer's summary is as follows:

■ the summary is imprinted with details of the retailer using a plastic card – the Retailer's Card – supplied with the imprinter machine

■ the amounts of the sales vouchers are listed on the reverse of the summary and totalled

■ the total is carried forward to the front of the summary

■ any refund vouchers are listed on the front of the summary

■ the summary is dated, signed and totalled

■ the summary is separated into its three copies – the top two are retained by the business and the bottom copy (the processing copy) is placed in front of the sales vouchers

■ the processing copy and sales and any refund vouchers are placed in a transparent envelope and are paid into the bank on a paying-in slip, the total from the summary listed as a single item on the paying-in slip

Businesses which accept sales by mail and telephone may use schedules rather than sales vouchers for recording and listing the credit card transactions. The procedure for paying-in for these businesses is exactly the same, except that the totals of the schedule(s) are listed on the back of the retailer summary rather than the individual amounts of the sales vouchers as described above.

As mentioned earlier, paper-based vouchers and summaries are becoming very rare as credit and debit card transactions are now transmitted electronically from card terminals and checkouts. This electronic process is faster, cheaper and far more efficient.

THE IMPORTANCE OF PAYING IN PROMPTLY

Businesses are well aware that problems can arise if money is not banked promptly and safely.

theft

Cash is tempting to a thief, and it must be remembered that many instances of theft are carried out by employees of a business rather than by criminals from the outside. A business will therefore have a security policy, for example:

- cash and cheques being paid in are kept under lock and key at the place of work, normally in a cash box, under the control of the cashier

- amounts received through the post or over the counter are recorded on remittance lists or on a cash register (or equivalent) as an additional security measure – money, once it is recorded, will be missed when stolen

- larger organisations will have a system of spot checking to identify any theft by employees

- arranging for cash and cheques to be taken to the bank by security firm (appropriate for large businesses)

- arranging for Friday and weekend takings of cash to be lodged in the bank's night safe

timescale – security and cashflow

Businesses will also have a policy for the prompt paying of money into the bank, for two main reasons – **security** and **cashflow**. Money kept on the premises is a security risk: the longer it remains there, the more likely it is that it will be stolen. Also, money not paid in is money that is not available for paying cheques and other items from the business's bank account: cashflow will be restricted. For example, it may be that the business is borrowing money on overdraft – it could save paying interest if money is banked promptly: a cheque for £100,000 lying around in the office for a week could cost the business a significant sum in lost interest!

procedures

Because of these factors a business will draw up procedures for banking money. These will include the security measures mentioned above and also set timescales for paying in money, eg twice a week. If you work in an accounts office, you may be familiar with these procedures.

confidentiality

If you work for an organisation, the importance of confidentiality will have been impressed on you. Confidentiality basically means not telling outsiders about the internal workings of your place of work. Important aspects of this include not talking to outsiders about your customers, not disclosing secret details of your products, and most importantly to this area of your studies, not disclosing your security arrangements for handling of money. Imagine the possible consequences of telling a group of friends that the cash security van calls at the bank every day at 12.00 noon.

AUTOMATED PAYMENTS INTO THE BANK

So far in this chapter we have looked at how a business pays into the bank manually, ie paying in on a paying-in slip. Many payments nowadays come into the bank account by computer transfer from other banks. The business can find out about these payments by:

■ receiving notification either through the post or by email

■ checking up-to-date account details through online banking

■ checking off the payments on the bank statement

A business enters details of cash and cheque payments in the accounts when the money is received. Payments received electronically must also be entered in the accounts when notification is received and checked in due course against the bank statement. The diagram below shows the variety of payments that can be received.

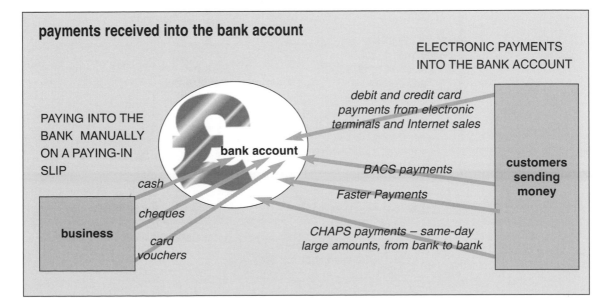

PAYMENTS THROUGH THE INTERNET

the process

If a business has an internet shopping facility, its customers order and pay for goods or services online using a credit or debit card and the money is credited direct to the bank account of the business. The business will receive a schedule of the payments received which it can check against its bank statement.

The diagram below shows the procedure adopted for this process. There is nothing significantly different from other payment systems about the way this system works – it is merely another way of providing a shopping outlet to customers with debit cards and credit cards.

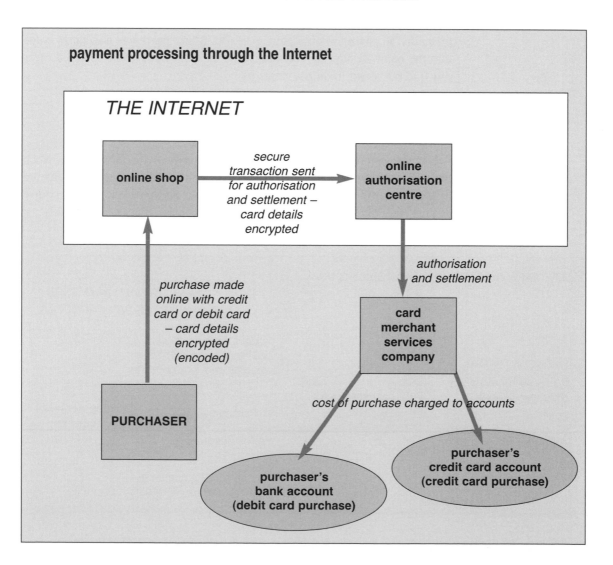

payment processing through the Internet

THE INTERNET

online shop

secure transaction sent for authorisation and settlement – card details encrypted

online authorisation centre

authorisation and settlement

purchase made online with credit card or debit card – card details encrypted (encoded)

card merchant services company

PURCHASER

cost of purchase charged to accounts

purchaser's bank account (debit card purchase)

purchaser's credit card account (credit card purchase)

As we noted in the last chapter, the buying public is concerned about the security of giving names, addresses and card numbers online. Businesses setting up selling facilities online have to make sure that the security of the system is maintained by using software which encodes the data (data 'encryption') so that payment details remain secret.

This security is no different in principle from the security measures adopted by businesses which accept debit and credit card payments over the counter, ie to keep any records of customers and their card numbers under lock and key, and not to throw any paper records of order forms with card numbers on in the bin where they can easily be found.

BANK STATEMENTS

At regular intervals the bank posts out statements of account to its customers or provides real-time statements online. A business current account with many items passing through it may have weekly paper statements, while a less active account or a deposit account may have monthly statements.

A bank statement is a summary showing:

■ the balance of the account at the beginning of the statement

■ amounts paid into the account

■ amounts paid out of the account – eg cheques issued, cheques returned 'unpaid', bank charges and standing orders and direct debits (automatic computer payments)

The balance of the account is shown after each transaction. A specimen bank statement is shown on the next page.

a note on debits, credits and bank accounts

You should be aware of the fact that the terms 'credit' and 'debit' mean different things to banks and their customers.

In the double-entry system of a business customer

debit = money received

credit = money paid out

Banks see things from the opposite side. To their accounting system:

debit = money paid out from a customer's account

credit = money paid into a customer's account

In other words a credit to an account from the bank's point of view is the same as a debit in the books of a customer. Think about it!

Albion Bank plc

7 The Avenue, Broadfield, BR1 2AJ

Account title	Trends	
Account number	11719512	
Statement	85	

Date	Details	Payments	Receipts	Balance
20-3				
3 Nov	Balance brought down			1,678.90 CR
10 Nov	Giro Credit 109626		1,427.85	3,106.75 CR
10 Nov	238628	249.57		2,857.18 CR
11 Nov	238629	50.00		2,807.18 CR
13 Nov	POS Streamline		67.45	2,874.63 CR
17 Nov	Giro Credit 109627		100.00	2,974.63 CR
17 Nov	Albionet Card Services POS 2824242		500.00	3,474.63 CR
21 Nov	238630	783.90		2,690.73 CR
24 Nov	238626	127.00		2,563.73 CR
24 Nov	Albionet Netsales 43182639		1,006.70	3,570.43 CR
25 Nov	BACS ORLANDO 37646		162.30	3,732.73 CR
25 Nov	DD Westmid Gas	167.50		3,565.23 CR
27 Nov	238634	421.80		3,143.43 CR
27 Nov	DD RT Telecom	96.50		3,046.93 CR
28 Nov	Bank charges	87.50		2,959.43 CR

checking the bank statement for payments received

You will see from the specimen bank statement shown above that the balance of the account is followed each time by the abbreviation 'CR'. This means that the customer has a credit balance, ie has money in the bank. The abbreviation 'DR' would indicate a debit balance – an overdraft, ie the customer would owe the bank money.

Note the following payments that have been received during the month:

- on 10 and 17 November the business has paid in on a paying-in slip
- on 13 November payment is received from debit card transactions
- on 17 November payment is received from credit card transactions
- on 24 November payment is received from Internet sales
- on 25 November payment is received via the BACS electronic transfer system – possibly a customer settling up an invoice

When a bank statement is received it should be checked and compared with the firm's record of bank receipts and payments – the cash book – and a bank reconciliation statement prepared (see the next chapter).

■ Organisations pay money into their bank account on a paying-in slip which lists the cash and cheques paid in and totals the amounts.

■ Cash and cheques must be checked and listed before they are paid in.

■ Credit and debit card vouchers may also be paid into the bank account on a retailer summary form which lists all of the vouchers.

■ Organisations should set up procedures to ensure that cash, cheques and card vouchers are kept safely on the premises and in transit to the bank.

■ Money should be paid into the bank as soon as possible, both for security reasons and also to help the cashflow of the business.

■ BACS, CHAPS, Faster Payments and card payments processed electronically over the counter and through the internet are also received into the bank account and advised to the business.

■ Businesses should keep records of automatically processed card payments secure for security reasons – card numbers are valuable to thieves.

■ Bank statements are provided to customers and should be checked regularly for manual and automatically processed payments received.

■ To a bank, money paid in is a 'credit' and money paid out is a 'debit'.

paying-in slip	a slip listing cash and cheques paid into a bank
retailer summary	a form listing credit card sales vouchers paid into a bank account
night safe	a wallet containing cash and cheques lodged with a bank through an opening in the wall of the bank
card merchant	a company which handles all the payments by debit card and credit card received by a business over the counter or through the Internet
encryption	the encoding for security reasons of debit and credit card details sent over the Internet
Faster Payments Service	same-day interbank electronic transfer system
BACS	Bankers Automated Clearing Services – used for sending computer payments from bank to bank
CHAPS	Clearing House Automated Payment System – used for sending same-day high value payments
bank statement	a document provided to its customer setting out transactions on the bank account

Activities

4.1 When checking a cheque for paying in at the bank and finding a problem, a business is able to alter the cheque by:

    (a)   adding the signature of the issuer (drawer) of the cheque if it is missing

    (b)   changing the amount in words if it is different from the amount in figures

    (c)   adding the date if it is missing

    (d)   changing the name of the payee if it is incorrect

Which one of these options is correct?

4.2 The firm you work for is Eveshore Traders Ltd., which has a bank account at Barclays Bank, Eveshore. You are required to prepare the paying-in slip and counterfoil (see below) as at today's date. The cheques are to be listed and totalled on the back of the paying-in slip.

The items to be banked are:

Cash	*Cheques*	
two £20 notes	£20.00	Maytree Enterprises
five £10 notes	£18.50	Bakewell Catering
eight £5 notes	£75.25	Henderson & Co
two £1 coins	£68.95	Musgrave Fine Art
six 50p coins		
four 10p coins		
two 2p coins		

Date _____	Date _____	**bank giro credit**	£50 notes		
Credit _____	Cashier's stamp and initials		£20 notes		
£50 notes		**Code no** 20 23 88	£10 notes		
£20 notes		**Bank** BARCLAYS	£5 notes		
£10 notes		**Branch** EVESHORE	£1 £2		
£5 notes			50p		
£1 £2		EVESHORE TRADERS LTD	20p		
50p		Credit	10p,5p		
20p		Account No. 90003174	Bronze		
10p,5p			Total Cash		
Bronze		Number of cheques Paid in by _____	Cheques etc		
Total Cash					
Cheques etc		Do not write below this line	£		
£		20-23-88 90003174 77			

Counterfoil	Cheques		
£		Carried over	£

4.3 The firm you work for is Buxton Fine Wines, which has a bank account at Western Bank, Grantminster. Using today's date you are required to prepare the Retailer Summary and paying-in slip for ten credit card sales vouchers and a refund voucher. The documents are shown below and on the next page. The items to be banked are:

Sales vouchers	£45.60	£56.85
	£10.00	£56.00
	£15.50	£45.00
	£25.99	£49.50
	£67.50	£25.00
Refund voucher	£13.50	

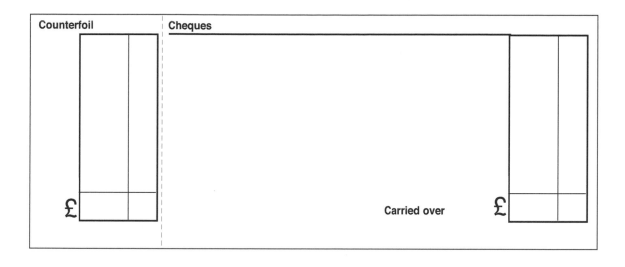

Date _____
Credit _____

£50 notes		
£20 notes		
£10 notes		
£5 notes		
£1 £2		
50p		
20p		
10p,5p		
Bronze		
Total Cash		
Cheques etc		
£		

Date _____
Cashier's stamp and initials

bank giro credit

Code no	47 21 95
Bank	WESTERN
Branch	GRANTMINSTER

Credit _____ BUXTON FINE WINES
Account No. _____ 87163729

Number of cheques

Paid in by _____

Do not write below this line

47 21 95   87163729   77

£50 notes		
£20 notes		
£10 notes		
£5 notes		
£1 £2		
50p		
20p		
10p,5p		
Bronze		
Total Cash		
Cheques etc		
£		

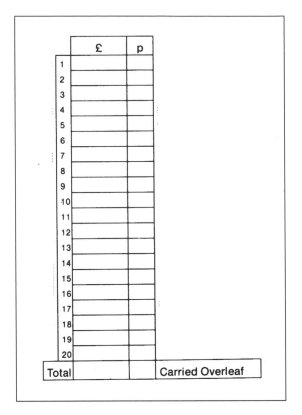

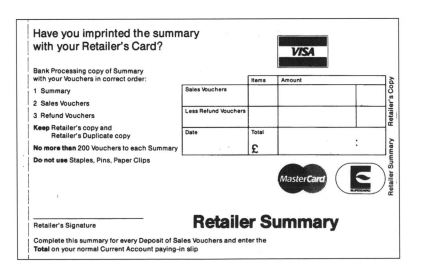

4.4 The firm you work for is Freshmead Limited, which has a bank account at Albion Bank, Broadfield.

You have just received the November bank statement, which is shown below.

Study the statement and answer the questions that follow.

Albion Bank plc
7 The Avenue, Broadfield, BR1 2AJ

Account title	Freshmead Limited
Account number	12098525
Statement	22

Date	Details	Payments	Receipts	Balance
20-3				
3 Nov	Balance brought down			2,678.90 CR
10 Nov	Giro Credit 173406		1,427.85	4,106.75 CR
10 Nov	712518	249.57		3,857.18 CR
11 Nov	712519	50.00		3,807.18 CR
13 Nov	Giro Credit 173407		67.45	3,874.63 CR
17 Nov	Giro Credit 173408		100.00	3,974.63 CR
17 Nov	BACS R Patel 98423		500.00	4,474.63 CR
21 Nov	712520	783.90		3,690.73 CR
24 Nov	712516	127.00		3,563.73 CR
24 Nov	Hermes Netsales 91879184		3,006.70	6,570.43 CR
25 Nov	BACS J Smith Ltd 37646		162.30	6,732.73 CR
25 Nov	DD Ion Power	167.50		6,565.23 CR
27 Nov	712524	421.80		6,143.43 CR
27 Nov	DD Mercury Telecom	96.50		6,046.93 CR
28 Nov	Bank charges	87.50		5,959.43 CR

(a) How much money is there in the account at the beginning of the month and at the end of the month?

(b) Identify the transactions which involve money being paid in on a paying in slip. What is the total paid in?

(c) Identify the transactions which involve cheques issued by Freshmead Limited. What is the total paid out in this way?

(d) Explain what the BACS items on 17 and 25 November are.

(e) What BACS direct debits have been paid out during the month?

(f) What money has been received from Freshmead's online sales for the month?

(g) The opening balance on 3 November is £2,678.90 CR. What would it mean if the statement had shown an opening balance of £2,678.90 DR? What effect would this have had on the bank balance during the month and how would this have been shown on the statement?

Bank reconciliation statements

this chapter covers...

The preparation of bank reconciliation statements requires a knowledge of:

- *bank statements - see page 69*
- *simple cash book - covered in the unit for Processing Bookkeeping Transactions*

The previous chapters have explained the various forms of receipts and payments that may be shown on a business bank statement. The business cash book was covered in Chapter 9 of Bookkeeping 1 Tutorial - for bank reconciliation statements it is the ability to update a simple cash book from the bank statement, and to total and balance the cash book, that is required.

The purpose of bank reconciliation statements is to form the link between the balance at bank shown in the cash book of a business bookkeeping system and the balance shown on the bank statement received from the bank.

The reasons why the cash book and bank statement may differ - and need reconciling - are because:

- *there are timing differences caused by:*

  - *unpresented cheques, ie the time delay between the business writing out a cheque and recording it in the cash book, and the cheque being entered by the bank on the bank statement*

  - *outstanding lodgements, ie amounts paid into the bank by the business, but not yet recorded on the bank statement*

- *the cash book has not been updated with items which appear on the bank statement and which should also appear in the cash book such as direct debits, standing orders and bank charges*

Assuming that there are no errors and both cash book and bank statement are correct, the two documents need to be reconciled with each other, ie their closing balances need to be agreed by means of a calculation known as a bank reconciliation statement.

RECEIVING THE BANK STATEMENT

When the bank statement is received it must be matched or compared with the cash book in order to identify any differences or discrepancies.

These differences are:

■ timing differences

■ updating items for the cash book

timing differences

The two main timing differences or discrepancies between the bank columns of the cash book and the bank statement are:

■ **unpresented cheques**, ie cheques issued, not yet recorded on the bank statement

■ **outstanding lodgements**, ie amounts paid into the bank, not yet recorded on the bank statement

The first of these – **unpresented cheques** – is caused because, when a cheque is written out, it is immediately entered on the payments side of the cash book, even though it may be some days before the cheque passes through the bank clearing system and is recorded on the bank statement. Therefore, for a few days at least, the cash book shows a lower balance than the bank statement in respect of this cheque. When the cheque is recorded on the bank statement, the difference will disappear. We have looked at only one cheque here, but a business will often be issuing several cheques each day, and the difference between the cash book balance and the bank statement balance may be considerable.

With the second timing difference – **outstanding lodgements** – the business's cashier will record a receipt in the cash book as he or she prepares the bank paying-in slip. However, the receipt may not be recorded by the bank on the bank statement for a day or so, particularly if it is paid in late in the day, or if it is paid in at a bank branch other than the one at which the account is maintained.

Until the receipt is recorded by the bank the cash book will show a higher bank account balance than the bank statement. Once the receipt is entered on the bank statement, the difference will disappear.

These two timing differences are involved in the calculation known as the **bank reconciliation statement**. The business cash book must not be altered because, as we have seen, they will correct themselves on the bank statement as time goes by.

updating items for the cash book

Besides the timing differences described on the previous page, there may be other differences between the bank columns of the cash book and the bank statement, and these do need to be entered in the cash book to bring it up-to-date.

For example, the bank might make an automatic standing order payment on behalf of a business – such an item is correctly deducted by the bank, and it might be that the bank statement acts as a reminder to the business cashier of the payment: it should then be entered in the cash book.

Examples of items that show in the bank statement and need to be entered in the cash book include:

receipts - money in

- credit transfers (BACS – Bankers Automated Clearing Services) amounts received by the bank, eg payments from trade receivables
- dividend amounts received by the bank
- bank interest received

payments - money out

- standing order and direct debit payments (many businesses keep schedules of their standing orders and direct debits – from these they write up the cash book as the payments fall due)
- bank charges and interest
- unpaid cheques deducted by the bank, for example, cheques from customers paid in by the business which have 'bounced' and are returned by the bank marked 'refer to drawer'

For each of these items, the cashier needs to check to see if they have been entered in the cash book; if not, they need to be recorded (provided that the bank has not made an error). If the bank has made an error, it must be notified as soon as possible and the incorrect transactions reversed by the bank in its own accounting records.

THE BANK RECONCILIATION STATEMENT

The **bank reconciliation statement** forms the link between the balances shown in the bank statement and in the cash book:

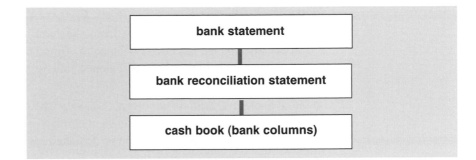

Upon receipt of a bank statement, reconciliation of the two balances is carried out in the following way:

■ tick off the items that appear in both cash book and bank statement

■ the unticked items on the bank statement are entered into the bank columns of the cash book to bring it up-to-date (provided none are errors made by the bank)

■ the bank columns of the cash book are now balanced to find the revised figure

■ the remaining unticked items from the cash book will be the timing differences

■ the timing differences are used to prepare the bank reconciliation statement, which takes the following format (with example figures):

XYZ TRADING LIMITED
Bank Reconciliation Statement as at 31 October 20-1

		£	£
Balance at bank as per bank statement			245
Less: unpresented cheques			
J Lewis	cheque no 0012378	60	
ABC Limited	cheque no 0012392	100	
Eastern Oil Company	cheque no 0012407	80	
		240	
			5
Add: outstanding lodgements		220	
		300	
			520
Balance at bank as per cash book			525

Notes:

- The layout shown above starts from the bank statement balance, and works towards the cash book balance. A common variation of this layout is to start with the cash book balance and to work towards the bank statement balance (see page 84).

- If a bank overdraft is involved, brackets should be used around the numbers to indicate this for the bank statement or cash book balance. The timing differences are still added or deducted, as appropriate.

- Once the bank reconciliation statement agrees, it should be filed because it proves that the bank statement and cash book were reconciled at a particular date. If, next time it is prepared, it fails to agree, the previous statement is proof that reconciliation was reached at that time.

Case Study

BANK RECONCILIATION STATEMENT

situation

The cashier of Severn Trading Company has written up the business's cash book for the month of February 20-1, as shown below.

Note that the cheque number is shown against payments.

Dr				Cash Book				Cr
Date	Details	Cash	Bank	Date	Details	Cash	Bank
20-1		£	£	20-1		£	£
2 Feb	Balances b/d	250.75	1,340.50	3 Feb	Appleton Ltd 123456		675.25
6 Feb	A Abbott		208.50	5 Feb	Wages	58.60	
10 Feb	Sales	145.25		12 Feb	Rent 123457		125.00
16 Feb	Sales		278.30	17 Feb	D Smith & Co 123458		421.80
20 Feb	Sales	204.35		24 Feb	Stationery	75.50	
23 Feb	D Richards Ltd		162.30	25 Feb	G Christie 123459		797.55
26 Feb	Sales		353.95		Balances c/d	466.25	586.25
27 Feb	P Paul Ltd		262.30				
		600.35	2,605.85			600.35	2,605.85
	Balances b/d	466.25	586.25				

The cash balance of £466.25 shown by the cash columns at the month-end has been agreed with the cash held in the cash box. The bank statement for February 20-1 has just been received:

National Bank plc
Bartown Branch

	Account title	Severn Trading Company
	Account number	67812318
	Statement	45

Date	Details	Payments	Receipts	Balance
20-1		£	£	£
2 Feb	Balance brought forward			1340.50 Cr
7 Feb	Credit		208.50	1549.00 Cr
10 Feb	Cheque 123456	675.25		873.75 Cr
17 Feb	Credit		278.30	1152.05 Cr
17 Feb	Cheque 123457	125.00		1027.05 Cr
24 Feb	Credit		162.30	1189.35 Cr
24 Feb	BACS J Jarvis Ltd		100.00	1289.35 Cr
26 Feb	Cheque 123458	421.80		867.55 Cr
26 Feb	Direct debit A-Z Finance	150.00		717.55 Cr
27 Feb	Credit		353.95	1071.50 Cr
27 Feb	Bank charges	10.00		1061.50 Cr

solution

Note that the bank statement is prepared from the bank's viewpoint: thus a credit balance shows that the customer is a payable of the bank, ie the bank owes the balance to the customer. In the customer's own cash book, the bank is shown as a debit balance, ie an asset.

As the month-end balance at bank shown by the cash book, £586.25, is not the same as that shown by the bank statement, £1,061.50, it is necessary to compare individual items in the cash book and on the bank statement for accuracy. The steps are:

1   Tick off the items that appear in both cash book and bank statement.

2   The unticked items on the bank statement are entered into the bank columns of the cash book to bring it up-to-date. These are:

  •   receipt   24 Feb   BACS credit, J Jarvis Limited £100.00

  •   payments   26 Feb   Direct debit, A-Z Finance £150.00

              27 Feb   Bank Charges, £10.00

In double-entry bookkeeping, the other part of the transaction will need to be recorded in the accounts.

3   The cash book is now balanced to find the revised balance:

Dr		£			£
20-1			**20-1**		
	Balance b/d	586.25	26 Feb	A-Z Finance	150.00
24 Feb	J Jarvis Ltd	100.00	27 Feb	Bank Charges	10.00
			28 Feb	Balance c/d	526.25
		686.25			686.25
1 Mar	Balance b/d	526.25			

Cash Book (bank columns) — Cr

4   The remaining unticked items from the cash book are:

   • receipt 27 Feb – P Paul Limited £262.30

   • payment 25 Feb – G Christie (cheque no 123459) £797.55

These items are timing differences, which should appear on next month's bank statement. They will be used in the bank reconciliation statement.

5   The bank reconciliation statement is now prepared, starting with the bank statement balance of £1,061.50 and using the unticked items from the cash book which were noted above.

SEVERN TRADING COMPANY
Bank Reconciliation Statement as at 28 February 20-1

	£
Balance at bank as per bank statement	1,061.50
Less: unpresented cheque, no 123459	797.55
	263.95
Add: outstanding lodgement, P Paul Limited	262.30
Balance at bank as per cash book	526.25

This bank reconciliation statement starts with the bank statement balance, and finishes with the amended balance from the cash book, ie the two figures are reconciled.

notes on the case study

• The unpresented cheque is deducted from the bank statement balance because, until it is recorded by the bank, the bank statement shows a higher balance than the cash book.

• The outstanding lodgement is added to the bank statement balance because, until it is recorded by the bank, the bank statement shows a lower balance than the cash book.

PREPARING A BANK RECONCILIATION STATEMENT

In order to help with the Activities at the end of the chapter, here is a step-by-step summary of the procedure. Reconciliation of the bank statement balance with that shown in the cash book should be carried out in the following way:

1   From the bank columns of the cash book tick off, in both cash book and bank statement, the receipts that appear in both.

2   From the bank columns of the cash book tick off, in both cash book and bank statement, the payments that appear in both.

3   Identify the items that are unticked on the bank statement and enter them in the cash book on the debit or credit side, as appropriate. (If, however, the bank has made a mistake and debited or credited an amount in error, this should not be entered in the cash book, but should be notified to the bank for them to make the correction. The amount will need to be entered on the bank reconciliation statement.)

4   The bank columns of the cash book are now balanced to find the up-to-date balance.

5   Start the bank reconciliation statement with the final balance figure shown on the bank statement.

6   In the bank reconciliation statement deduct the unticked payments shown in the cash book – these will be unpresented cheques.

7   In the bank reconciliation statement, add the unticked receipts shown in the cash book – these are outstanding lodgements.

8   The resulting money amount shown on the bank reconciliation statement is the balance at bank as per the cash book.

The layout which is often used for the bank reconciliation statement is that shown in the Case Study on the previous page. The layout starts with the bank statement balance and finishes with the cash book balance. However, there is no reason why it should not commence with the cash book balance and finish with the bank statement balance: with this layout it is necessary to:

■ *add* unpresented cheques

■ *deduct* outstanding lodgements

The bank reconciliation statement of Severn Trading Company would then appear as (see the next page):

SEVERN TRADING COMPANY
Bank Reconciliation Statement as at 28 February 20-1

	£
Balance at bank as per cash book	526.25
Add: unpresented cheque, no 123459	797.55
	1,323.80
Less: outstanding lodgement, P Paul Limited	262.30
Balance at bank as per bank statement	1,061.50

DEALING WITH UNUSUAL ITEMS ON BANK STATEMENTS

The following are some of the unusual features that may occur on bank statements. As with other accounting discrepancies, where they cannot be resolved they should be referred to the accounts supervisor for guidance.

out-of-date cheques

These are cheques that are more than six months old. The bank will not pay such cheques, so they can be written back in the cash book, ie debit cash book (and credit the other double-entry account involved).

returned (dishonoured) cheques

A cheque received by a business is entered as a receipt in the cash book and then paid into the bank, but it may be returned ('bounced') by the drawer's (issuer's) bank to the payee's bank because:

- the drawer (the issuer) has stopped it
- the cheque has been returned by the bank, either because the drawer has no money (a 'dishonoured' cheque) or because there is a technical problem with the cheque, eg it is not signed

A cheque returned in this way should be entered in the bookkeeping system:

- as a payment in the cash book on the credit side, and
- – either as a debit to sales ledger control account (if it is a credit sale), and a debit to the trade receivable's account in sales ledger
  - or as a debit to sales account (if it is a cash sale)

bank errors

Errors made by the bank can include:

- **a cheque deducted from the bank account which has not been issued by the business** – look for a cheque number on the bank statement that is different from the current cheque series: take care, though, as it could be a cheque from an old cheque book

■ **a BACS receipt shown on the bank statement for which the business is not the correct recipient**; if in doubt, the bank will be able to give further details of the sender of the money

■ **standing orders and direct debits paid at the wrong time or for the wrong amounts**; a copy of all standing order and direct debit mandates sent to the bank should be kept by the business for reference purposes, standing order and direct debit schedules should be kept up-to-date so that the cash book can be written up as the payments fall due

When an error is found, it should be queried immediately with the bank. The item and amount should not be entered in the business's cash book until it has been resolved. If, in the meantime, a bank reconciliation statement is to be prepared, the bank error should be shown separately. When the reconciliation is from the bank statement balance to the cash book balance, add payments and deduct receipts that the bank has applied to the account incorrectly.

bank interest received

For certain types of accounts banks may pay interest to their customers. When this happens the bank statement of the customer shows a receipt for 'interest received' or 'bank interest received'.

bank charges and interest paid

From time-to-time banks charge customers' accounts with an amount for:

– service charges, ie the cost of operating the bank account

– interest paid, ie the borrowing cost when the bank account is overdrawn

On a bank statement, such items are shown in the 'payments' or 'paid out' column.

RECONCILIATION OF OPENING CASH BOOK AND BANK STATEMENT BALANCES

If you look back to the Case Study on pages 80-82, you will see that both the cash book (bank columns) and the bank statement balance both started the month with the same balance: 1 February 20-1 £1,340.50.

In reality, it is unlikely that the opening cash book and bank statement balances will be the same. It will be necessary, in these circumstances, to prepare a simple opening bank reconciliation statement in order to prove that there are no errors between cash book and bank statement at the start of the month.

This is set out in the same format as the end-of-month bank reconciliation statement, and is best prepared immediately after ticking off the items that appear in both cash book and bank statement. The earliest unpresented cheques drawn and outstanding lodgements will, most probably, be causing the difference. Of course, where last month's bank reconciliation statement is available, such as in business, there is no need to prepare an opening reconciliation.

There is usually no need to prepare a formal opening bank reconciliation statement as any discrepancy in opening balances can be resolved quickly by checking the bank statement for the earliest receipts and payments.

IMPORTANCE OF BANK RECONCILIATION STATEMENTS

- A bank reconciliation statement is important because, in its preparation, the transactions in the bank columns of the cash book are compared with those recorded on the bank statement. In this way, any errors in the cash book or bank statement will be found and can be corrected (or advised to the bank, if the bank statement is wrong).

- The bank statement is an independent accounting record, therefore it will assist in deterring fraud by providing a means of verifying the cash book balance.

- By writing the cash book up-to-date, the business has an amended figure for the bank balance to be shown in the trial balance.

- It is good business practice to prepare a bank reconciliation statement each time a bank statement is received. The reconciliation statement should be prepared as quickly as possible so that any queries – either with the bank statement or in the cash book – can be resolved. Many businesses will specify to their accounting staff the timescales for preparing bank reconciliation statements – as a guideline, if the bank statement is received weekly, then the reconciliation statement should be prepared within five working days.

Chapter Summary

- The purpose of a bank reconciliation statement is to reconcile the balance shown by the bank statement with that shown by the bank columns of the cash book.

- Certain differences between the two are timing differences. The main timing differences are:
  - unpresented cheques
  - outstanding lodgements

  These differences will be corrected by time and, most probably, will be recorded on the next bank statement.

- ◼ Certain differences appearing on the bank statement need to be entered in the cash book to bring it up-to-date. These include:

  Receipts   – credit transfer (BACS) amounts received by the bank

              – dividend amounts received by the bank

              – bank interest

  Payments   – standing order and direct debit payments

              – bank charges and interest

              – unpaid cheques debited by the bank

- ◼ The bank reconciliation statement makes use of the timing differences.

- ◼ Once prepared, a bank reconciliation statement is proof that the bank statement and the cash book (bank columns) were agreed at a particular date.

Key Terms

bank reconciliation statement	forms the link between the balances shown in the bank statement and the cash book
timing differences	discrepancies between the bank statement and the cash book that will be corrected over time, such as unpresented cheques and outstanding lodgements
unpresented cheques	cheques drawn, but not yet recorded on the bank statement
outstanding lodgements	amounts paid into the bank, but not yet recorded on the bank statement
direct debit/standing order schedules	lists of direct debit and standing order payments, kept by a business, from which the cash book is written up as payments fall due

Activities

5.1 When preparing a bank reconciliation statement, which one of the following is a timing difference?

(a)   unpresented cheques

(b)   direct debit payments

(c)   bank charges and interest

(d)   BACS receipts

Answer (a) or (b) or (c) or (d)

5.2 A business's bank statement shows a balance of £400 in the bank. Unpresented cheques total £350; outstanding lodgements total £200. What is the balance at bank shown by the cash book?

(a)   £100 credit

(b)   £200 debit

(c)   £250 debit

(d)   £400 debit

Answer (a) or (b) or (c) or (d)

5.3 The bank columns of Tom Reid's cash book for December 20-2 are as follows:

20-2	Receipts		£	20-2	Payments		£
1 Dec	Balance b/d		280	9 Dec	W Smith	345123	40
13 Dec	P Jones		30	13 Dec	Rent	345124	50
17 Dec	H Homer		72	16 Dec	Wages	345125	85
29 Dec	J Hill		13	20 Dec	B Kay	345126	20
				31 Dec	Balance c/d		200
			395				395

He then received his bank statement which showed the following transactions for December 20-2:

BANK STATEMENT		Payments	Receipts	Balance
20-2		£	£	£
1 Dec	Balance brought forward			280 CR
13 Dec	Credit		30	310 CR
15 Dec	Cheque no 345123	40		270 CR
17 Dec	Cheque no 345124	50		220 CR
22 Dec	Credit		72	292 CR
23 Dec	Cheque no 345125	85		207 CR

You are to prepare a bank reconciliation statement which agrees the bank statement balance with the cash book balance.

5.4 The bank columns of P Gerrard's cash book for January 20-3 are as follows:

20-3	Receipts	£	20-3	Payments		£
1 Jan	Balance b/d	800.50	2 Jan	A Arthur Ltd	001351	100.00
6 Jan	J Baker	495.60	9 Jan	C Curtis	001352	398.50
30 Jan	G Shotton Ltd	335.75	13 Jan	Donald & Co	001353	229.70
			14 Jan	Bryant & Sons	001354	312.00
			23 Jan	P Reid	001355	176.50

He received his bank statement which showed the following transactions for January 20-3:

BANK STATEMENT		Payments	Receipts	Balance
20-3		£	£	£
1 Jan	Balance brought forward			800.50 CR
6 Jan	Cheque no 001351	100.00		700.50 CR
6 Jan	Credit		495.60	1,196.10 CR
13 Jan	BACS credit: T K Supplies		716.50	1,912.60 CR
20 Jan	Cheque no 001352	398.50		1,514.10 CR
23 Jan	Direct debit: Omni Finance	207.95		1,306.15 CR
26 Jan	Cheque no 001353	229.70		1,076.45 CR
31 Jan	Bank interest		5.50	1,081.95 CR

You are to:

(a) check the items on the bank statement against the items in the cash book and update the cash book accordingly; total the cash book and show the balance carried down at 31 January 20-3

(b) prepare a bank reconciliation statement at 31 January 20-3 which agrees the bank statement balance with the cash book balance

5.5 The bank columns of Jane Doyle's cash book for May 20-4 are as follows:

20-4	Receipts	£	20-4	Payments		£
1 May	Balance b/d	300	3 May	P Stone	867714	28
7 May	Cash	162	14 May	Alpha Ltd	867715	50
17 May	C Brewster	89	28 May	E Deakin	867716	110
27 May	Cash	60				
28 May	Cash	40				

She received her bank statement which showed the following transactions for May 20-4:

BANK STATEMENT		Payments	Receipts	Balance
20-4		£	£	£
1 May	Balance brought forward			400 CR
2 May	Cheque no 867713	100		300 CR
5 May	Cheque no 867714	28		272 CR
7 May	Credit		162	434 CR
17 May	Standing order: A-Z Insurance	25		409 CR
19 May	Credit		89	498 CR
20 May	Cheque no 867715	50		448 CR
27 May	Credit		60	508 CR
31 May	Bank Charges	10		498 CR

You are to:

(a) write the cash book up-to-date at 31 May 20-4, and show the balance carried down

(b) prepare a bank reconciliation statement at 31 May 20-4 which agrees the bank statement balance with the cash book balance

5.6 On 4 June Milestone Motors received a bank statement which showed the following transactions for May 20-5:

BANK STATEMENT		Paid out	Paid in	Balance
20-5		£	£	£
1 May	Balance brought forward			3,802 C
2 May	Cheque no 451761	150		3,652 C
10 May	Cheque no 451762	751		2,901 C
11 May	Cheque no 451763	268		2,633 C
13 May	Cheque no 451765	1,045		1,588 C
14 May	BACS credit: Perran Taxis		2,596	4,184 C
18 May	Direct debit: Wyvern Council	198		3,986 C
20 May	Direct debit: A1 Insurance	1,005		2,981 C
25 May	Direct debit: Okaro and Company	254		2,727 C
25 May	Bank charges	20		2,707 C
D = Debit C = Credit				

The cash book of Milestone Motors as at 31 May 20-5 is shown below:

CASH BOOK

Date	Details	Bank	Date	Cheque no	Details	Bank
20-5		£	20-5			£
1 May	Balance b/f	3,652	4 May	451762	Smith and Company	751
26 May	J Ackland	832	4 May	451763	Bryant Limited	268
28 May	Stamp Limited	1,119	7 May	451764	Curtis Cars	1,895
			7 May	451765	Parts Supplies	1,045

You are to:

(a) check the items on the bank statement against the items in the cash book

(b) update the cash book as needed

(c) total the cash book and show clearly the balance carried down at 31 May and brought down at 1 June

(d) prepare a bank reconciliation statement at 31 May 20-5 which agrees the bank statement balance with the cash book balance

5.7 On 30 June Durning Trading received a bank statement as at 27 June 20-8:

BANK STATEMENT		Paid out	Paid in	Balance
20-8		£	£	£
1 Jun	Balance brought forward			768 C
4 Jun	Cheque 364125	427		341 C
5 Jun	BACS credit: Asif Ltd		1,122	1,463 C
18 Jun	Cheque 364127	4,200		2,737 D
20 Jun	Direct debit: JC Property Co	850		3,587 D
23 Jun	BACS credit: Sand & Stone		2,486	1,101 D
26 Jun	BACS credit: Surfrider Ltd		4,110	3,009 C
27 Jun	Direct debit: Vord Finance	275		2,734 C
27 Jun	Cheque 364128	1,062		1,672 C
D = Debit C = Credit				

The cash book of Durning Trading as at 27 June 20-8 is shown below:

CASH BOOK

Date	Details	Bank	Date	Cheque no	Details	Bank
20-8		£	20-8			£
1 Jun	Balance b/d	1,890	1 Jun	364125	Penryn Ltd	427
20 Jun	Chiverton Ltd	1,200	3 Jun	364126	Fal Boats	760
24 Jun	Perran Ltd	4,750	10 Jun	364127	S Mawes	4,200
24 Jun	P Porth	8,950	20 Jun	364128	Castle Supplies	1,062

You are to:

(a) check the items on the bank statement against the items in the cash book

(b) update the cash book as needed

(c) total the cash book and clearly show the balance carried down at 27 June and brought down at 28 June

(d)   using the form below, prepare a bank reconciliation statement as at 27 June which agrees the bank statement balance with the cash book balance (note: not all the lines may be needed)

Bank reconciliation statement as at 27 June 20-8	
Balance as per bank statement	£
Add	
Name:	£
Name:	£
Name:	£
Name:	£
Total to add	£
Less	
Name:	£
Name:	£
Name:	£
Name:	£
Total to subtract	£
Balance as per cash book	£

6 Using control accounts

this chapter covers...

In this chapter we look at control accounts which are used as 'master' accounts to control a number of subsidiary accounts.

A control account (also known as a totals account) is used to record the total of transactions passing through the subsidiary accounts. In this way, the balance of the control account will always be equal (unless an error has occurred) to the total balances of the subsidiary accounts.

The three control accounts we will study in this chapter are:

■ sales ledger control account – the total of trade receivables

■ purchases ledger control account – the total of trade payables

■ Value Added Tax control account – the total of VAT due to or from HM Revenue & Customs

The chapter explains:

■ the general purpose of control accounts

■ how control accounts work

■ reconciling control accounts to subsidiary accounts

■ the layout of control accounts

■ how control accounts fit into the accounting system

■ information sources for control accounts

THE GENERAL PURPOSE OF CONTROL ACCOUNTS

Control accounts are 'master' accounts which control a number of subsidiary accounts – individual supplier or customer accounts – for example. This set-up can be illustrated as follows:

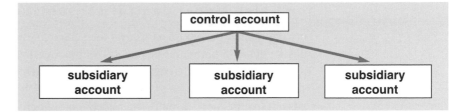

The control account (also known as a **totals account**) is used to record the totals of transactions passing through the subsidiary accounts. In this way, the balance of the control account will always be equal to the total balances of the subsidiary accounts, unless an error has occurred.

Three commonly-used control accounts in an accounting system are:

- **sales ledger control account**, which controls the sales ledger
- **purchases ledger control account**, which controls the purchases ledger
- **Value Added Tax control account**, which brings together totals of VAT from books of prime entry, such as the day books and cash book

Note: each of these control accounts is a general ledger account in the accounting system.

In the illustration above we have seen how a control account acts as a master account for a number of subsidiary accounts. The principle is that, if the total of the opening balances for subsidiary accounts is known, together with the total of amounts increasing these balances, and the total of amounts decreasing these balances, then the total of the closing balances for the subsidiary accounts can be calculated.

For example:

	£
Total of opening balances	50,000
Add increases	10,000
	60,000
Less decreases	12,000
Total of closing balances	48,000

The total of the closing balances can now be reconciled (agreed) against a separate listing of the balances of the subsidiary accounts to ensure that the two figures agree. If they do, it proves that the ledgers within the section are correct, unless an error has occurred within the ledger section.

SALES LEDGER CONTROL ACCOUNT

how sales ledger control account works

The diagram on the next page shows the subsidiary accounts which form the sales ledger of a particular business – in practice there would be more than four trade receivables' (customers') accounts involved. The sales ledger control account acts as a totals account, which records totals of the transactions passing through the accounts which it controls. Note that transactions are shown in the control account **on the same side** as in the subsidiary accounts.

Sales ledger control account is reconciled with the balances of the subsidiary accounts which it controls. Thus, control accounts act as an aid to locating errors: if the control account and subsidiary accounts agree, then the error is likely to lie elsewhere. In this way the control account acts as an intermediate checking device – proving the arithmetical accuracy of the ledger section unless an error has occurred within the ledger section.

importance of reconciling sales ledger control account

At regular intervals – eg weekly or monthly – it is important that a business reconciles the balances of subsidiary accounts in sales ledger with the balance of sales ledger control account. To carry out this reconciliation, the balances of the subsidiary accounts in sales ledger are listed and then totalled – the total should agree with the balance of sales ledger control account. Any discrepancy (see page 103) should be investigated immediately and the error(s) traced.

Using the accounts shown on the next page the sales ledger control account and the subsidiary sales ledger accounts will be reconciled at the beginning and end of the month, as follows:

Reconciliation of sales ledger control account		
	1 January 20-4	*31 January 20-4*
	£	£
A Ackroyd	100	150
B Barnes	200	200
C Cox	50	180
D Douglas	150	150
Sales ledger control account	500	680

GENERAL LEDGER

Dr			Sales Ledger Control Account		Cr
20-4		£	20-4		£
1 Jan	Balance b/d	500	31 Jan	Bank	443
31 Jan	Sales	700	31 Jan	Discount allowed	7
			31 Jan	Sales returns	70
			31 Jan	Balance c/d	680
		1,200			1,200
1 Feb	Balance b/d	680			

SALES LEDGER

Dr			A Ackroyd		Cr
20-4		£	20-4		£
1 Jan	Balance b/d	100	12 Jan	Bank	98
6 Jan	Sales	150	12 Jan	Discount allowed	2
			31 Jan	Balance c/d	150
		250			250
1 Feb	Balance b/d	150			

Dr			B Barnes		Cr
20-4		£	20-4		£
1 Jan	Balance b/d	200	13 Jan	Bank	195
6 Jan	Sales	250	13 Jan	Discount allowed	5
			27 Jan	Sales returns	50
			31 Jan	Balance c/d	200
		450			450
1 Feb	Balance b/d	200			

Dr			C Cox		Cr
20-4		£	20-4		£
1 Jan	Balance b/d	50	20 Jan	Bank	50
15 Jan	Sales	200	29 Jan	Sales returns	20
			31 Jan	Balance c/d	180
		250			250
1 Feb	Balance b/d	180			

Dr			D Douglas		Cr
20-4		£	20-4		£
1 Jan	Balance b/d	150	30 Jan	Bank	100
20 Jan	Sales	100	31 Jan	Balance c/d	150
		250			250
1 Feb	Balance b/d	150			

sales ledger control account explained

The layout of the sales ledger control account is shown below, with sample figures.

Study the layout carefully and then read the text which follows:

Dr		Sales Ledger Control Account		Cr
	£			£
Balance b/d	2,900	Cash/cheques received from customers		12,100
Credit sales	14,000	Settlement (cash) discount allowed		290
Returned cheques	930	Sales returns		870
		Irrecoverable debts written off		1,590
		Set-off/contra entries		250
		Balance c/d		2,730
	17,830			17,830
Balance b/d	2,730			

balance b/d

The figure for balance b/d on the debit side of the control account represents the total of the balances of the individual trade receivables' accounts in the sales ledger. This principle has been seen in the diagram on page 97. Remember that, at the end of the month (or other period covered by the control account), the account must be balanced and carried down (on the credit side) on the last day of the month, and then brought down (on the debit side) on the first day of the next month.

Note that it is possible for a customer's account to have a credit balance, instead of the usual debit balance. This may come about, for example, because the customer has paid for goods and then returned them, or has overpaid in error: the business owes the amount due, ie the customer has a credit balance for the time being. Most accounting systems 'net off' any such credit balances against the debit balances to give an overall figure for trade receivables.

credit sales

Only credit sales – and not cash sales – are entered in the control account because only credit sales are recorded in the customers' accounts. However, the total sales of a business may well comprise both credit and cash sales.

dishonoured cheques

If a customer's cheque is dishonoured – returned unpaid – by the bank, ie the cheque has 'bounced', then authorisation for the entries to be made in the accounting system must be given by the accounts supervisor. These entries are:

– *debit* sales ledger control account

– *credit* cash book (bank columns)

The transaction must also be recorded in the customer's account in the sales ledger – on the debit side.

Note that the returned cheque is the prime document for the adjustment – like other prime documents it should be stored securely for future reference.

irrecoverable (bad) debts written off

An irrecoverable (bad) debt is a debt owing to a business which it considers will never be paid.

We will look in more detail at irrecoverable debts written off in the next chapter. For the moment the accounting entries after a debt has been authorised for write off are:

– *debit* irrecoverable debts account

– *credit* sales ledger control account

The transaction must also be recorded in the customer's account in sales ledger – on the credit side.

set-off/contra entries

These entries occur when the same person or business has a subsidiary account in both the sales ledger and the purchases ledger, ie they are both buying from, and selling to, the business whose accounts we are preparing.

Set-off contra entries are looked at in more detail on page 110, where we will see the entries which affect the control accounts.

sales ledger control account in the accounting system

The diagram on the next page shows how sales ledger control account is incorporated in the general ledger of the accounting system, with the trade receivables' accounts kept as subsidiary accounts in sales ledger.

- Sales ledger control account is part of the double-entry system
- Customer accounts are in sales ledger as subsidiary accounts

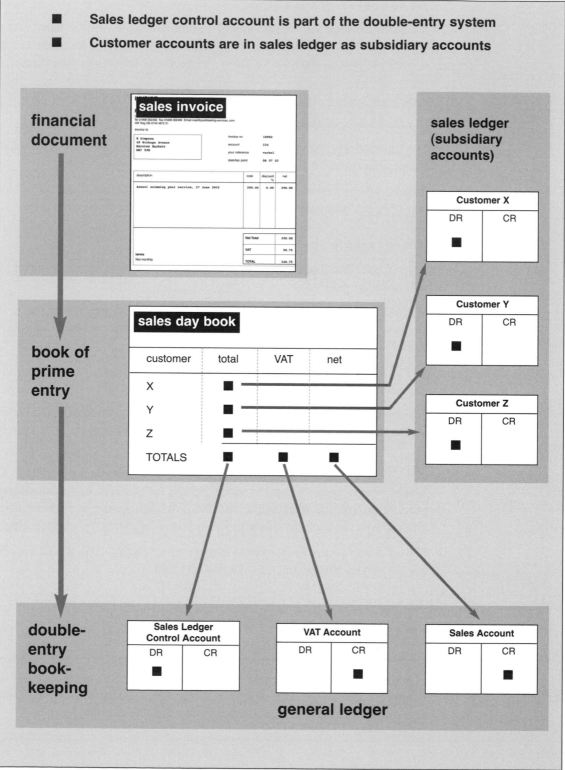

From time-to-time, the balances of the sales ledger subsidiary accounts are reconciled with the balance of sales ledger control account, and any discrepancies investigated.

information sources for sales ledger control account

Control accounts use totals (remember that their other name is 'totals accounts') for the week, month, quarter or year – depending on what time period is decided upon by the business. The totals for sales ledger control account come from a number of sources in the accounting system:

- total credit sales (including VAT) – from the 'total' column of the sales day book

- total sales returns (including VAT) – from the 'total' column of the sales returns day book

- total cash/cheques received from customers – from the analysed cash book

- total settlement discount allowed – from the discount allowed column of the cash book, or from discount allowed account

- irrecoverable debts – from the journal, or irrecoverable debts written off account (see Chapter 7)

using an aged trade receivables analysis

An **aged trade receivables analysis** is a summary of each trade receivable balance from sales ledger analysed into columns showing how long the amounts have been outstanding. It is used by a business to show which customers are slow in paying and enables the business to decide which customers to chase for payment.

An example of an aged trade receivables analysis is given below.

Wyvern Trading Aged trade receivables analysis at 30 September 20-6				
Trade receivable	Total	0-30 days	31-60 days	61+ days
	£	£	£	£
Adams Ltd	3,510	0	0	3,510
T Brewster	1,840	1,620	220	0
Harrison & Co	760	760	0	0
D Miller	2,330	330	2,000	0
Totals	8,440	2,710	2,220	3,510

An aged trade receivables analysis can either be drawn up manually, or it can be printed out from a computer accounting package.

The analysis is normally produced at the end of each month when statements are sent out to customers. From the analysis (see previous page) the business decides which customers it is going to chase up, and how. It may send a letter, an email, or it may telephone the customer. For example, from the above aged trade receivables analysis, the account of Adams Ltd is overdue for payment and a strongly worded letter, followed up with a telephone call might be needed; most of the balance of D Miller's account is now overdue and a letter or email might be sent as a reminder; the account of T Brewster is partly overdue but it is unlikely that any action will be taken this month; the account of Harrison & Co is 'in order'.

dealing with discrepancies

As stated earlier, it is important at regular intervals to reconcile the balances of subsidiary accounts in sales ledger with the balance of sales ledger control account. The diagram on the opposite page shows where error(s) might occur. The first thing to do is to establish:

- is the balance of sales ledger control account greater than the total of the balances of the subsidiary accounts in sales ledger?

   or

- is the total of the balances of the subsidiary accounts in sales ledger greater than the balance of sales ledger control account?

Once this has been established, the relevant column from the diagram indicates what may have caused the discrepancy. The discrepancy can then be investigated, the error(s) traced and any problems solved quickly and professionally.

PURCHASES LEDGER CONTROL ACCOUNT

how purchases ledger control account works

The diagram on page 104 shows the personal accounts which form the purchases ledger of a particular business – in practice there would be more than four trade payables' (suppliers') accounts involved.

Purchases ledger control account acts as a totals account, which records totals of the transactions passing through the subsidiary accounts which it controls. Note that transactions are shown in the control account on the same side as in the subsidiary accounts.

continued on page 104

Discrepancies between sales ledger control account (slca) and sales ledger (sl)		
possible discrepancy	slca greater than sl	sl greater than slca
credit sales		
– omitted/understated in slca	✗	✔
– omitted/understated in sl	✔	✗
– entered twice/overstated in slca	✔	✗
– entered twice/overstated in sl	✗	✔
sales returns		
– omitted/understated in slca	✔	✗
– omitted/understated in sl	✗	✔
– entered twice/overstated in slca	✗	✔
– entered twice/overstated in sl	✔	✗
money received from trade receivables		
– omitted/understated in slca	✔	✗
– omitted/understated in sl	✗	✔
– entered twice/overstated in slca	✗	✔
– entered twice/overstated in sl	✔	✗
settlement (cash) discount		
– omitted/understated in slca	✔	✗
– omitted/understated in sl	✗	✔
– entered twice/overstated in slca	✗	✔
– entered twice/overstated in sl	✔	✗
irrecoverable debts written off		
– omitted/understated in slca	✔	✗
– omitted/understated in sl	✗	✔
– entered twice/overstated in slca	✗	✔
– entered twice/overstated in sl	✔	✗
other		
– debit balance recorded in error as credit in sl	✔	✗
– credit balance recorded in error as debit in sl	✗	✔

GENERAL LEDGER

Dr	Purchases Ledger Control Account					Cr
20-4		£	20-4			£
31 Jan	Purchases returns	150	1 Jan	Balance b/d		1,000
31 Jan	Bank	594	31 Jan	Purchases		1,700
31 Jan	Discount received	6				
31 Jan	Balance c/d	1,950				
		2,700				2,700
			1 Feb	Balance b/d		1,950

PURCHASES LEDGER

Dr	F Francis					Cr
20-4		£	20-4			£
16 Jan	Bank	98	1 Jan	Balance b/d		100
16 Jan	Discount received	2	2 Jan	Purchases		200
31 Jan	Balance c/d	200				
		300				300
			1 Feb	Balance b/d		200

Dr	G Gold					Cr
20-4		£	20-4			£
15 Jan	Purchases returns	50	1 Jan	Balance b/d		200
28 Jan	Bank	100	9 Jan	Purchases		300
31 Jan	Balance c/d	350				
		500				500
			1 Feb	Balance b/d		350

Dr	H Harris					Cr
20-4		£	20-4			£
28 Jan	Purchases returns	100	1 Jan	Balance b/d		300
30 Jan	Bank	200	16 Jan	Purchases		500
31 Jan	Balance c/d	500				
		800				800
			1 Feb	Balance b/d		500

Dr	I Ingram					Cr
20-4		£	20-4			£
22 Jan	Bank	196	1 Jan	Balance b/d		400
22 Jan	Discount received	4	27 Jan	Purchases		700
31 Jan	Balance c/d	900				
		1,100				1,100
			1 Feb	Balance b/d		900

importance of reconciling purchases ledger control account

At regular intervals – eg weekly or monthly – it is important that a business reconciles the balances of subsidiary accounts in purchases ledger with the balance of purchases ledger control account. To carry out this reconciliation, the balances of the subsidiary accounts in purchases ledger are listed and then totalled – the total should agree with the balance of purchases ledger control account. Any discrepancy should be investigated immediately and the error(s) traced.

From the diagram on the previous page the purchases ledger control account and the subsidiary purchases ledger accounts will be reconciled at the beginning and end of the month, as follows:

Reconciliation of purchases ledger control account		
	1 January 20-4	*31 January 20-4*
	£	£
F Francis	100	200
G Gold	200	350
H Harris	300	500
I Ingram	400	900
Purchases ledger control account	1,000	1,950

purchases ledger control account explained

The layout of the purchases ledger control account is shown below, with sample figures.

Study the layout carefully and then read the text on the next page.

Dr		**Purchases Ledger Control Account**		Cr
	£			£
Cash/cheques paid to suppliers	8,200	Balance b/d		5,000
Settlement (cash) discount received	260	Credit purchases		8,500
Purchases returns	1,070			
Set-off/contra entries	250			
Balance c/d	3,720			
	13,500			13,500
		Balance b/d		3,720

balance b/d

The figure for balance b/d on the credit side of the control account represents the total of the balances of the individual trade payables' accounts in the purchases ledger. This principle has been seen in the diagram on page 104.

Note that it is possible for a supplier's account to have a debit balance, instead of the usual credit balance. This may come about, for example, if the supplier has been overpaid. Most accounting systems 'net off' any such debit balances against the credit balances to give an overall figure for suppliers.

credit purchases

Only credit purchases – and not cash purchases – are entered in the control account because only credit purchases are recorded in the suppliers' accounts. However, the total purchases of a business may well comprise both credit and cash purchases.

set-off/contra entries

These entries occur when the same person or business has a subsidiary account in both the purchases ledger and the sales ledger, ie they are both selling to, and buying from, the business whose accounts we are preparing.

Set-off/contra entries are looked at in more detail in the next section, where we will see the entries which affect the control accounts.

purchases ledger control account in the accounting system

The diagram on the next page shows how purchases ledger control account is incorporated in the general ledger of the accounting system, with the trade payables' accounts kept as subsidiary accounts in the purchases ledger.

From time-to-time, the balances of the purchases ledger subsidiary accounts are agreed with the balance of purchases ledger control account, and any discrepancies investigated.

- Purchases ledger control account is part of the double-entry system
- Suppliers' accounts are in purchases ledger as subsidiary accounts

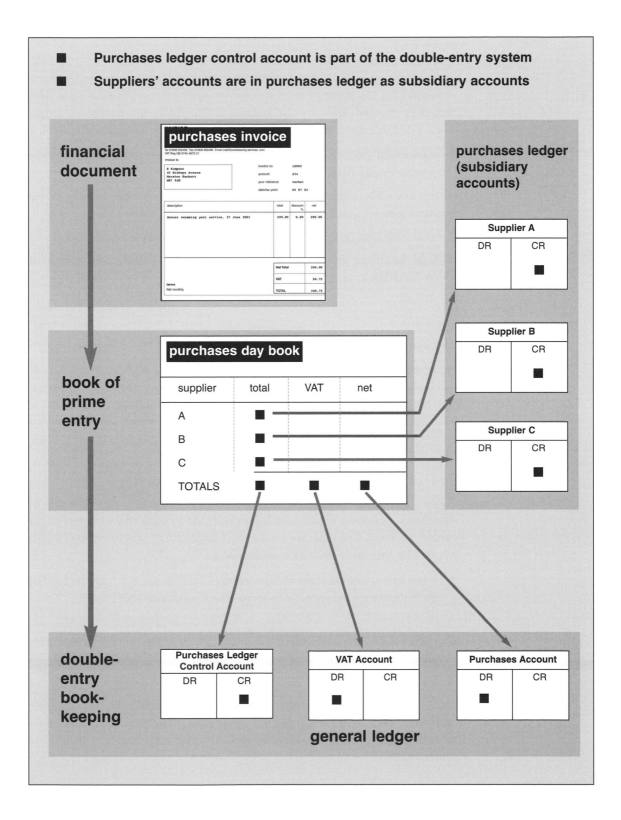

information sources for purchases ledger control account

Control accounts use totals (remember that their other name is totals accounts) for the week, month, quarter or year – depending on what time period is decided upon by the business. The totals for purchases ledger control account come from a number of sources in the accounting system:

- total credit purchases (including VAT) – from the 'total' column of the purchases day book

- total purchases returns (including VAT) – from the 'total' column of the purchases returns day book

- total cash/cheques paid to suppliers – from the analysed cash book

- total settlement discount received – from the discount received column of the cash book, or from discount received account

using an aged trade payables analysis

An **aged trade payables analysis** works in the same way as an aged trade receivables analysis (see page 101), except that it is a summary of each trade payable balance. It is used by a business to show how long accounts have been outstanding and it enables the business to decide which suppliers to pay.

dealing with discrepancies

As we have seen earlier, it is important to reconcile the balances of subsidiary accounts in purchases ledger with the balance of purchases ledger control account. The diagram on the next page shows where error(s) might occur. The first thing to do is to establish:

- is the balance of purchases ledger control account greater than the total of the balances of the subsidiary accounts in purchases ledger?

  or

- is the total of the balances of the subsidiary accounts in purchases ledger greater than the balance of purchases ledger control account?

Once this has been established, the relevant column from the diagram indicates what may have caused the discrepancy. The discrepancy can then be investigated, the error(s) traced and any problems solved quickly and professionally.

Discrepancies between purchases ledger control account (plca) and purchases ledger (pl)		
possible discrepancy	plca greater than pl	pl greater than plca
credit purchases		
– omitted/understated in plca	✗	✔
– omitted/understated in pl	✔	✗
– entered twice/overstated in plca	✔	✗
– entered twice/overstated in pl	✗	✔
purchases returns		
– omitted/understated in plca	✔	✗
– omitted/understated in pl	✗	✔
– entered twice/overstated in plca	✗	✔
– entered twice/overstated in pl	✔	✗
money paid to trade payables		
– omitted/understated in plca	✔	✗
– omitted/understated in pl	✗	✔
– entered twice/overstated in plca	✗	✔
– entered twice/overstated in pl	✔	✗
settlement (cash) discount		
– omitted/understated in plca	✔	✗
– omitted/understated in pl	✗	✔
– entered twice/overstated in plca	✗	✔
– entered twice/overstated in pl	✔	✗
other		
– credit balance recorded in error as debit in pl	✔	✗
– debit balance recorded in error as credit in pl	✗	✔

SET-OFF/CONTRA ENTRIES

These entries occur when the same person or business has a subsidiary account in both sales ledger and purchases ledger, ie they are both buying from, and selling to, the business whose accounts we are preparing. For example, Patel Limited has the following accounts in the sales and purchases ledgers:

SALES LEDGER

Dr		A Smith		Cr
		£		£
Balance b/d		200		

PURCHASES LEDGER

Dr		A Smith		Cr
		£		£
			Balance b/d	300

From these accounts we can see that:

■ A Smith owes Patel Limited £200 (sales ledger)

■ Patel Limited owes A Smith £300 (purchases ledger)

To save each having to make a bank payment to the other, it is possible (with A Smith's agreement) to set-off one account against the other, so that they can settle their net indebtedness with one bank payment. The bookkeeping entries in Patel's books will be:

– *debit* A Smith (purchases ledger) £200

– *credit* A Smith (sales ledger) £200

The accounts will now appear as:

SALES LEDGER

Dr		A Smith		Cr
		£		£
Balance b/d		200	Set-off: purchases ledger	200

PURCHASES LEDGER

Dr		£	A Smith	Cr	£
Set-off: sales ledger		200	Balance b/d		300

The net result is that Patel Limited owes A Smith £100. The important point to note is that, because transactions have been recorded in the subsidiary ledger accounts, an entry needs to be made in the two control accounts:

– *debit* purchases ledger control account

– *credit* sales ledger control account

Set-off transactions should be appropriately documented and authorised.

VALUE ADDED TAX (VAT) CONTROL ACCOUNT

how VAT control account works

VAT control account brings together totals of VAT from books of prime entry, such as the day books and cash book. The diagram on page 112 shows how VAT control account fits into the accounting system.

It is from VAT control account that the VAT Return is prepared, checked and then submitted online to HM Revenue & Customs – often quarterly, ie every three months. VAT Return shows:

- either, the money amount due to be paid by the business when VAT collected from sales is greater than the VAT paid on purchases

- or, the money amount due as a refund from HM Revenue & Customs to the business when VAT collected from sales is less than the VAT paid on purchases

verifying VAT control account

Whilst VAT control account does not have subsidiary accounts in sales or purchases ledger to reconcile against, it is nevertheless a totals account. The VAT amounts must be recorded from the books of prime entry; the balance of VAT control account tells the business how much is due to or from HM Revenue & Customs. The account balance must be verified with the amount shown on the business VAT Return – any discrepancy should be investigated immediately and the error(s) traced.

VAT control account explained

A typical layout of a VAT control account with sample figures is shown below. Study the layout carefully and then read the text which follows.

Dr		VAT Control Account		Cr
	£			£
Purchases	30,000	Sales		40,000
Sales returns	1,500	Purchases returns		1,000
Cash purchases	4,000	Cash sales		5,000
Other cash expenses	700	Other cash income		300
Balance c/d	10,100			
	46,300			46,300
		Balance b/d		10,100

purchases

This is the amount of VAT taken from the totals row of purchases day book, which is the VAT paid by the business on its credit purchases.

sales returns

Here is recorded the amount of VAT taken from the totals row of sales returns day book. This is the VAT allowed back to customers of the business on the sales returns they make.

cash purchases and other cash expenses

The total of the VAT column from the payments side of cash book is debited to VAT control account. This total will comprise VAT paid on the cash purchases of the business, including other expenses – both capital and revenue – paid for as cash transactions.

sales

This is the amount of VAT taken from the totals row of sales day book, which is the VAT calculated by the business on its credit sales.

purchases returns

Here is recorded the amount of VAT taken from the totals row of purchases returns day book. This is the VAT allowed back to the business by its suppliers on purchases returns.

continued on page 114

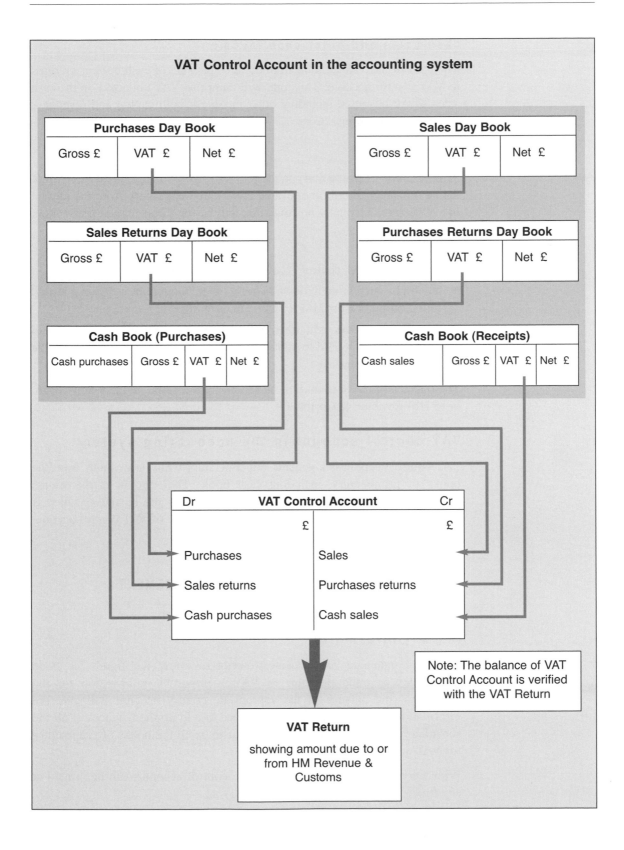

VAT Control Account in the accounting system

cash sales and other cash income

The total of the VAT column from the receipts side of cash book is credited to VAT control account. This total will comprise VAT collected on the cash sales of the business, including other income – both capital and revenue – received as cash transactions.

the journal

Another book of prime entry is the journal – which is discussed in detail in the next chapter. From time-to-time there may be an entry from the journal to VAT control account – however this will be for a non-regular transaction.

balance

The balance on VAT control account can be either debit or credit:

- a debit balance brought down indicates that the amount is due as a refund to the business from HM Revenue & Customs
- a credit balance brought down indicates that the amount is due to be paid by the business to HM Revenue & Customs (which is the situation for the majority of businesses)

The balance of the account will be settled with a bank payment either from or to HM Revenue & Customs.

VAT control account in the accounting system

VAT control account is a general ledger account which uses totals from the books of prime entry, including cash book. The account is the source information for preparation of the VAT Return of the business, which is submitted to HM Revenue & Customs. The balance of VAT control account must be verified with the VAT Return.

CONTROL ACCOUNTS AS AN AID TO MANAGEMENT

instant information

When the manager of a business needs to know the figure for trade receivables or trade payables or VAT – important information for the manager – the balance of the appropriate control account will give the information immediately. There is no need to add up the balances of all the subsidiary customer/supplier accounts, or to go to the books of prime entry for VAT amounts.

With a computer accounting system, the control accounts can be printed at any time.

prevention of fraud

The use of control accounts makes fraud more difficult – particularly in a manual accounting system. If a fraudulent transaction is to be recorded on a subsidiary account, the transaction must also be entered in the control account. As the control account will be either maintained by a supervisor, or checked regularly by the manager, the control accounts add another level of security within the accounting system. In most accounting systems, staff are only able to access the accounting information appropriate to their work.

location of errors

Control accounts can also help in locating errors. Remember, though, that a control account only proves the arithmetical accuracy of the accounts which it controls – there could still be errors within the subsidiary ledger section.

limitation of control accounts

Whilst control accounts can help in locating errors, they do have the limitation that not all errors will be shown. For example, if a transaction is entered into the wrong trade receivable's subsidiary account within sales ledger, this will not be revealed when the control account is reconciled to the subsidiary accounts.

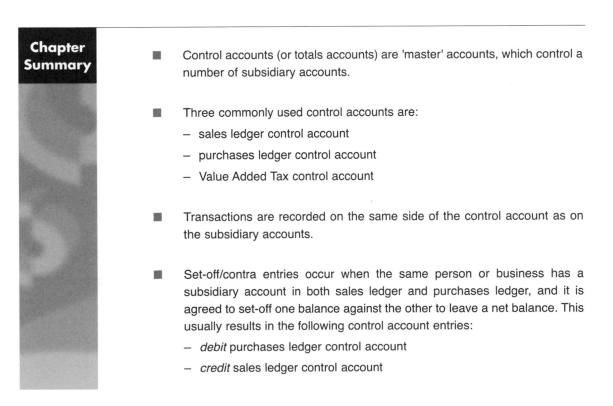

Chapter Summary

- Control accounts (or totals accounts) are 'master' accounts, which control a number of subsidiary accounts.

- Three commonly used control accounts are:
  - sales ledger control account
  - purchases ledger control account
  - Value Added Tax control account

- Transactions are recorded on the same side of the control account as on the subsidiary accounts.

- Set-off/contra entries occur when the same person or business has a subsidiary account in both sales ledger and purchases ledger, and it is agreed to set-off one balance against the other to leave a net balance. This usually results in the following control account entries:
  - *debit* purchases ledger control account
  - *credit* sales ledger control account

- In most accounting systems, control accounts are incorporated into the general ledger of the double-entry bookkeeping system. The subsidiary accounts are in separate ledgers – sales ledger and purchases ledger.

- At regular intervals control accounts are reconciled as follows:
  - sales ledger control account to the total of the balances of the subsidiary accounts in sales ledger
  - purchases ledger control account to the total of the balances of the subsidiary accounts in purchases ledger
  - VAT control account to the amount due to or from HM Revenue & Customs

- Control accounts are an aid to management:
  - they give instant information on the total of trade receivables/trade payables/VAT
  - by making fraud more difficult
  - in helping to locate errors (but not all errors will be shown)

Key Terms		
control account	a 'master' account which controls a number of subsidiary accounts
sales ledger control account	the general ledger account which controls the sales ledger
purchases ledger control account	the general ledger account which controls the purchases ledger
Value Added Tax control account	the account which brings together totals of VAT from the books of prime entry
set-off/contra entries	where balances in the sales ledger and the purchases ledger are set-off against one another
aged trade receivables' analysis	a summary of each customer balance analysed into columns showing how long the amounts have been outstanding

Activities

6.1 You have the following information:

- opening customer balances at start of month   £18,600
- credit sales for month   £9,100
- sales returns for month   £800

What is the figure for closing customer balances at the end of the month?

(a)   £10,300

(b)   £26,900

(c)   £27,700

(d)   £28,500

Answer (a) or (b) or (c) or (d)

6.2 Prepare a sales ledger control account for the month of June 20-7 from the following information:

20-7		£
1 Jun	Debit balance brought down	17,491
30 Jun	Credit sales for month	42,591
	Sales returns from credit customers	1,045
	Money received from credit customers	39,024

Balance the account at 30 June 20-7.

6.3 You work as an accounts assistant for Shire Traders. Today you are working on the sales ledger control account and sales ledger.

A summary of transactions with credit customers during June 20-5 is shown below.

	£
Goods sold on credit	118,600
Money received from credit customers	96,214
Discounts allowed	300
Goods returned by credit customers	650
Irrecoverable debt written off	350

The balance of customer accounts at 1 June 20-5 was £180,824.

(a)   Prepare a sales ledger control account for the month of June 20-5 from the above details. Show clearly the balance carried down at 30 June 20-5.

Sales Ledger Control Account

Date 20-5	Details	Amount £	Date 20-5	Details	Amount £

The following subsidiary account balances were in the sales ledger on 30 June 20-5:

	£	
Carless and Company	76,560	debit
BBT Limited	28,109	debit
Dale and Company	32,019	debit
Vale Computers	1,645	debit
Brandon Limited	350	debit
Bissell and Bradley	31,304	debit
Hopkins and Company	32,273	debit

(b)   Reconcile these balances with the sales ledger control account balance you calculated in (a).

	£
Sales ledger control account balance as at 30 June 20-5	. . . .
Total of sales ledger accounts as at 30 June 20-5	. . . .
Difference	. . . .

(c)   What may have caused the difference calculated in (b)?

....

....

....

6.4   You work as an accounts assistant for Southtown Supplies. Today you are working on the sales ledger control account and sales ledger.

A summary of transactions with credit customers in September 20-2 is shown below.

(a)   Show with a tick whether each entry will be a debit or credit in the sales ledger control account in the general ledger.

	Amount £	Debit ✔	Credit ✔
Balance of credit customers at 1 September 20-2	47,238		
Goods sold to credit customers	31,054		
Money received from credit customers	29,179		
Goods returned by credit customers	2,684		
Discounts allowed	784		
Irrecoverable debt written off	450		

(b)   What will be the balance of credit customers on 1 October 20-2 on the above account?

	✔
£44,295	
£45,195	
£45,645	
£46,095	

(c)   The balances in the sales ledger on 1 October 20-2 totalled £44,728

What is the difference between the total of the balances in the sales ledger and the sales ledger control account balance calculated in part (b)?

£
Workings:

(d)   Identify the two reasons, either of which might have caused the difference.

	✔
Settlement discount has been understated in the sales ledger	
Goods returned have been understated in the sales ledger	
The irrecoverable debt written off has been omitted from the sales ledger	
Money received from customers has been overstated in the sales ledger	
Sales to credit customers have been overstated in the sales ledger	
Sales to credit customers have been understated in the sales ledger	
Trade discounts have not been included in the sales ledger	

6.5   You work as an accounts assistant for Bransford Supplies. Today, 2 April 20-8, you have printed out the aged trade receivables analysis as at 31 March 20-8, as follows:

Bransford Supplies Aged trade receivables analysis at 31 March 20-8				
Customer	Total	0-30 days	31-60 days	61+ days
	£	£	£	£
Benn Ltd	2,430	630	1,800	0
Charteris & Co	1,760	1,760	0	0
D Morgan	940	820	120	0
Wilson & Sons	3,610	0	0	3,610
Totals	8,740	3,210	1,920	3,610

The trade terms of Bransford Supplies are 'net 30 days'.

For each of the customer accounts listed, indicate the action you suggest should be taken by the accounts supervisor.

	no action ✔	letter/email ✔	letter/email + phone call ✔
Benn Ltd			
Charteris & Co			
D Morgan			
Wilson & Sons			

6.6   You have the following information:

- opening supplier balances at start of month   £15,300
- credit purchases for month   £8,100
- purchases returns for month   £200

What is the figure for closing supplier balances at the end of the month?

(a)   £7,000

(b)   £7,400

(c)   £23,200

(d)   £23,600

Answer (a) or (b) or (c) or (d)

6.7   Prepare a purchases ledger control account for the month of April 20-9 from the following information:

20-9		£
1 Apr	Credit balance brought down	14,275
30 Apr	Credit purchases for month	36,592
	Purchases returns to credit suppliers	653
	Payments made to credit suppliers	31,074
	Contra entry (set-off against sales ledger control account)	597

Balance the account as at 30 April 20-9.

6.8   You work as an accounts assistant for Durning Traders. Today you are working on the purchases ledger control account and purchases ledger.

A summary of transactions with credit suppliers during May 20-3 is shown below.

	£
Goods purchased on credit	21,587
Payments made to credit suppliers	13,750
Discounts received	500
Goods returned to credit suppliers	250

The balance of suppliers at 1 May 20-3 was £50,300.

(a) Prepare a purchases ledger control account for the month of May 20-3 from the above details. Show clearly the balance carried down at 31 May 20-3.

Purchases Ledger Control Account

Date 20-3	Details	Amount £	Date 20-3	Details	Amount £

The following subsidiary account balances were in the purchases ledger on 31 May 20-3:

Wright and Company	£12,000	credit
CCY Limited	£11,107	credit
Carter and Company	£9,380	credit
Tomkins Limited	£16,800	credit
PP Properties	£500	debit
L Vakas	£1,200	credit
Ten Traders	£6,400	credit

(b) Reconcile these balances with the purchases ledger control account balance you calculated in (a).

	£
Purchases ledger control account balance as at 31 May 20-3	. . . .
Total of purchases ledger accounts as at 31 May 20-3	. . . .
Difference	. . . .

(c)   What may have caused the difference calculated in (b)?

....

....

....

6.9 You work as an accounts assistant for Mawla Supplies. Today you are working on the purchases ledger control account and purchases ledger.

A summary of transactions with credit suppliers during August 20-4 is shown below.

(a)   Show whether each entry will be a debit or credit in the purchases ledger control account in the general ledger.

	Amount £	Debit ✔	Credit ✔
Balance of credit suppliers at 1 August 20-4	46,297		
Purchases from credit suppliers	22,084		
Payments made to credit suppliers	25,934		
Discounts received	425		
Goods returned to credit suppliers	1,108		

(b)   What will be the balance of credit suppliers on 1 September 20-4 on the above account?

	✔
£41,764	
£48,614	
£43,130	
£40,914	

The following credit balances were in the purchases ledger on 1 September 20-4.

	£
Perran Ltd	5,340
Chiverton & Co	2,195
Durning Builders	11,084
Chapelporth Ltd	7,319
Sennen & Co	3,107
Zelah plc	10,861

(c)   Reconcile the balances shown above with the purchases ledger control account balance calculated in part (b).

£

Balance on purchases ledger control account at 1 September 20-4	
Total of the purchases ledger balances at 1 September 20-4	
Difference	

(d)   Which one of the following errors may have caused the difference calculated in part (c)?

✔

An invoice was entered twice in the purchases ledger	
A credit note was not entered in the purchases ledger	
A credit note was entered twice in the purchases ledger control account	
A credit note was not entered in the purchases ledger control account	

6.10   Indicate whether the following will be recorded as debits or credits in VAT control account:

	debit ✔	credit ✔
VAT on credit purchases		
VAT on cash sales		
VAT on purchases returns		
VAT on credit sales		
VAT on sales returns		

6.11 You work as an accounts assistant for Blenheim Builders. Today you are working on the VAT control account.

The following figures have been taken from Blenheim Builders' books of prime entry for the three months ended 30 June 20-4:

Sales day book	
Net	£56,000
VAT	£11,200
Gross	£67,200

Purchases day book	
Net	£23,200
VAT	£4,640
Gross	£27,840

Sales returns day book	
Net	£1,440
VAT	£288
Gross	£1,728

Purchases returns day book	
Net	£1,120
VAT	£224
Gross	£1,344

Cash book: cash sales	
Net	£2,480
VAT	£496
Gross	£2,976

(a) From the books of prime entry, write up the VAT control account of Blenheim Builders for the three months ended 30 June 20-4.

VAT Control Account

Date 20-4	Details	Amount £	Date 20-4	Details	Amount £

(b) Balance VAT control account at 30 June 20-4 and show the balance brought down on 1 July 20-4.

(c) The VAT Return calculation has been completed by another accounts assistant and shows an amount owing to HM Revenue & Customs of £7,280.

Is the VAT Return correct?   Yes/No

If it is not correct, what do you think has caused the error?

7 The journal

this chapter covers...

The journal is the book of prime entry for non-regular accounting transactions. Like other books of prime entry – eg sales day book – the journal is used to list transactions before they are entered into the double-entry bookkeeping system.

In this chapter we will see how the journal is maintained for non-regular transactions such as:

■ *opening entries (the first transactions to open the accounts of a new business)*

■ *irrecoverable debt write off (where a customer's account is to be written off)*

■ *payroll transactions (the accounting entries which record wages and salaries paid to employees)*

A further use of the journal is to show the entries required to correct errors found in the accounting system – this topic of correction of errors is covered in the next chapter.

MAINTAINING THE JOURNAL

The journal completes the accounting system by providing the book of prime entry for non-regular transactions which are not recorded in any other book of prime entry. Such non-regular transactions include:

■ opening entries

■ irrecoverable debt written off

■ payroll transactions

■ correction of errors (see Chapter 8)

The reasons for maintaining the journal are:

■ to provide a book of prime entry for non-regular transactions

■ to eliminate the need for remembering why non-regular transactions were put through the accounts – the journal acts as a notebook

■ to reduce the risk of fraud, by making it difficult for unauthorised transactions to be entered in the accounting system

■ to reduce the risk of errors, by listing the transactions that are to be put into the double-entry accounts

■ to ensure that entries can be traced back to an authorised financial document (note that documentation is stored securely for possible future reference)

THE JOURNAL – A BOOK OF PRIME ENTRY

The journal is a book of prime entry; it is not, therefore, part of the double-entry bookkeeping system. The journal lists the transactions that are to be put through the accounts. The accounting system for non-regular transactions is as follows:

The journal is set out in the following way, with a sample transaction:

Date	Details	Reference	Dr	Cr
20-4			£	£
1 Jul	Bank	CB	20,000	
	Capital	GL		20,000
	Opening capital introduced			

Notes:

- journal entries are prepared from authorised financial documents (which are stored securely for possible future reference)
- the names of the accounts to be debited and credited in the accounting system are written in the details column; it is customary to show the debit transaction first
- the money amount of each debit and credit entry is stated in the appropriate column
- the reference column shows where each account is found, and often includes an account number (eg CB = Cash Book, GL = General Ledger)
- a journal entry always balances, ie debit and credit entries are for the same amount or total
- it is usual to include a brief narrative (ie a few words) explaining why the transaction is being carried out, and making reference to the financial document whenever possible (you should always include a narrative unless specifically told otherwise)
- each journal entry is complete in itself and is ruled off to separate it from the next entry

Note that any transactions involving sales ledger control account and purchases ledger control account must also be recorded in the subsidiary accounts in sales ledger and purchases ledger respectively.

OPENING ENTRIES

Opening entries are the transactions to open the accounts of a new business.

An example of an opening entry is:

1 Jan 20-4 Started in business with £10,000 in the bank

This non-regular transaction is entered in the journal as follows:

Date	Details	Reference	Dr	Cr
20-4			£	£
1 Jan	Bank	CB	10,000	
	Capital	GL		10,000
	Opening capital introduced			

After the journal entry has been made, the transaction is recorded in the double-entry accounts, as follows:

GENERAL LEDGER

Dr	**Cash Book**					Cr		
20-4	Details	Cash	Bank	20-4	Details		Cash	Bank
		£	£				£	£
1 Jan	Capital		10,000					

Dr	**Capital Account**		Cr
20-4	£	20-4	£
		1 Jan Bank	10,000

Here is another opening entries transaction to be recorded in the journal:

1 Feb 20-4   *Started in business with cash £100, bank £5,000, inventory £1,000, machinery £2,500, trade payables £850*

The journal entry is:

Date	Details	Reference	Dr	Cr
20-4			£	£
1 Feb	Cash	CB	100	
	Bank	CB	5,000	
	Inventory	GL	1,000	
	Machinery	GL	2,500	
	Purchases ledger control	GL		850
	Capital*	GL		7,750
			8,600	8,600
	Assets and liabilities			
	at the start of business			

* Assets – liabilities = capital (ie 100 + 5,000 + 1,000 + 2,500 – 850 = 7,750)

Notes:

- capital is, in this example, the balancing figure, ie assets minus liabilities
- the journal is the book of prime entry for all opening entries, including cash and bank; however the normal book of prime entry for other cash/bank transactions is the cash book
- the amounts for the journal entry will now need to be recorded in the double-entry accounts as follows:

GENERAL LEDGER

Dr					Cash Book			Cr
20-4	Details	Cash	Bank	20-4	Details		Cash	Bank
		£	£				£	£
1 Feb	Capital	100	5,000					

Dr			Inventory Account		Cr
20-4			£	20-4	£
1 Feb	Capital		1,000		

Dr			Machinery Account		Cr
20-4			£	20-4	£
1 Feb	Capital		2,500		

Dr		Purchases Ledger Control Account			Cr
20-4		£	20-4		£
			1 Feb	Capital	850

Dr		Capital Account			Cr
20-4		£	20-4		£
			1 Feb	Journal	7,750

- the individual amounts making up the £850 recorded in purchases ledger control account must be recorded in the subsidiary accounts in purchases ledger
- the cross-reference in capital account is to the journal – in this way it is possible to refer back to the journal entry to see the assets and liabilities which formed the opening capital of the business; alternatively, individual amounts of the opening assets and liabilities could be recorded in capital account and cross-referenced with the name of their general ledger account

IRRECOVERABLE DEBTS WRITTEN OFF

An irrecoverable debt is a debt owing to a business which it considers will never be paid.

One of the problems of selling goods and services on credit terms is that, from time-to-time, some trade receivables will not pay. As a consequence, the balances of such trade receivables' accounts have to be written off when they become irrecoverable (uncollectable). This happens when all efforts to recover the amounts owing have been exhausted, ie statements and letters have been sent to the customer requesting payment, and legal action – where appropriate – or the threat of legal action, has failed to obtain payment.

In writing off a trade receivable's account as irrecoverable, the business is bearing the cost of the amount due. The account is written off and the amount is debited to irrecoverable debts written off account.

Towards the financial year-end it is good practice for the accounts supervisor (or other authorised person) to go through the trade receivables' accounts to see if any need to be written off. The accounts supervisor will then advise the accounts assistant which accounts are to be written off (the advice – often in the form of an email – forms the prime document for the irrecoverable debt write off).

We have already seen, in Chapter 6, the double-entry bookkeeping entries to write off a trade receivable's account:

- *debit* irrecoverable debts account
- *debit* Value Added Tax account
- *credit* sales ledger control account (and credit the subsidiary account of the customer in sales ledger)

For example:

15 Dec 20-4   *The accounts supervisor emails you telling you to write off the account of Don's Diner, which has a balance of £48 (including VAT), as an irrecoverable debt*

The journal entry is:

Date	Details	Reference	Dr	Cr
20-4			£	£
15 Dec	Irrecoverable debts	GL	40	
	Value Added Tax	GL	8	
	Sales ledger control	GL		48
			48	48
	Balance of subsidiary sales			
	ledger account of Don's Diner			
	written off as an irrecoverable debt,			
	as per email from accounts supervisor			

After the journal entry has been made, the transaction is recorded in the double-entry accounts as follows:

GENERAL LEDGER

Dr		**Irrecoverable Debts Account**		Cr
20-4		£	20-4	£
15 Dec	Sales ledger control	40		

Dr		**Value Added Tax Account**		Cr
20-4		£	20-4	£
15 Dec	Sales ledger control	8		

Dr		**Sales Ledger Control Account**		Cr
20-4		£	20-4	£
			15 Dec Irrecoverable debts/VAT	48

In sales ledger, the subsidiary account of Don's Diner is recorded as follows:

SALES LEDGER

Dr		**Don's Diner**		Cr
20-4		£	20-4	£
1 Dec	Balance b/d	48	15 Dec Irrecoverable debts/VAT	48

With the irrecoverable debt written off, this account now has a nil balance.

PAYROLL TRANSACTIONS

what is meant by payroll transactions?

Payroll transactions are the accounting entries which record wages and salaries paid to employees.

Payroll transactions require journal and accounting entries for:

– gross pay
– net pay
– income tax
– employer's National Insurance contributions
– employees' National Insurance contributions
– employer's pension contributions
– employees' pension contributions
– voluntary deductions from employees' pay

what payroll transactions are entered in the accounts?

The payroll transactions to be entered into the accounts are:

■ **gross pay**, which is the amount of employees' pay before any deductions

■ **net pay**, which is the amount paid to employees after deductions for income tax, employees' National Insurance contributions, employees' pension fund contributions and voluntary deductions

■ **income tax** collected by the employer and paid to HM Revenue & Customs

■ **employer's National Insurance** contributions paid to HM Revenue & Customs

■ **employees' National Insurance** contributions collected by the employer and paid to the HM Revenue & Customs

■ **pension contributions provided by the employer** and paid to pension funds

■ **employees' pension contributions** deducted from employees' pay and paid to pension funds

■ **voluntary deductions**, eg trade union fees, deducted from employees' pay and paid to the organisation

accounts used in payroll transactions

The double-entry accounts used to record payroll transactions are:

bank

This records:

■ payment of the net pay of employees

■ payment to outside agencies – the deductions to HM Revenue & Customs, payments to pension funds, and payments for voluntary deductions

wages control account

This is the main account for payroll – all transactions for payroll pass through this account which forms one-half of the double-entry – a debit or credit to wages control account will be a credit or debit in one of the other payroll accounts

wages expense

This is the employer's expense account for paying employees which records:

■ employees' gross pay

■ employer's National Insurance Contributions

■ employer's pension and voluntary contributions (if there are any)

HM Revenue & Customs

This records amounts payable to HM Revenue & Customs for income tax and National Insurance contributions

pension fund

This records amounts payable to external pension funds: the employer's and employees' contributions

wages control account

The diagram below shows the relationship of wages control account and the other payroll accounts. Note that the bank account is not shown here – it is involved in many of the transactions, as we will see in the Case Study on the next page.

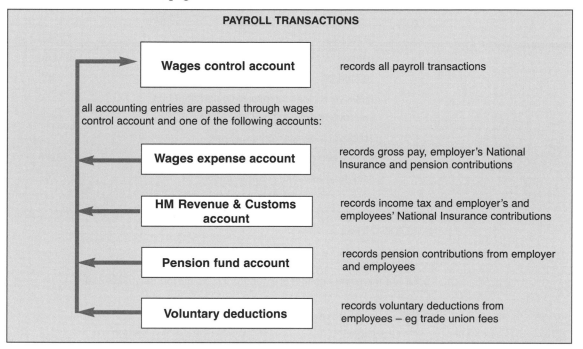

journal and ledger entries

Payroll transactions must be recorded by means of a journal entry in order to be able to trace the accounting entries from the payroll records (the financial document), through the book of prime entry (the journal) to the general ledger accounts.

As payroll is quite complex it is best to take a step-by-step approach (which is used in the Case Study on the next page). The journal entries and ledger entries are as follows:

1. Record the wages expense (the total cost to the employer)
2. Record the net pay (to be paid to employees)
3. Record the liability to HM Revenue & Customs (for income tax and National Insurance contributions)
4. Record the liability to the pension fund (both employer and employee contributions)
5. Record the liability for voluntary deductions, eg trade union fees

The Case Study which follows illustrates this step-by-step approach.

PAYROLL TRANSACTIONS

situation

Matrix is a small business employing five staff. It operates a monthly payroll which is run on the last day of the month. Payroll figures for November 20-8 are:

gross pay	£5,500
net pay	£3,820
income tax	£900
employer's National Insurance contributions	£550
employees' National Insurance contributions	£450
employer's pension contributions	£275
employees' pension contributions	£275
voluntary deductions: trade union fees	£55

We will now see the journal and general ledger entries for these payroll transactions, taking a step-by-step approach.

solution

These are the payments that are due for the November payroll of Matrix.

payments due to the employees

Gross pay	£5,500	
less		
Income tax	£900	
National Insurance	£450	
Pension contributions	£275	
Trade union fees	£55	
Net pay due		£3,820

payment due to HM Revenue & Customs

Income tax deducted from pay	£900	
Employer's National Insurance contributions	£550	
Employees' National Insurance contributions	£450	
		£1,900

payment due to the pension fund

Employer's contributions	£275	
Employees' contributions, deducted from pay	£275	
		£550

payment due to voluntary deductions

Employees' payment, for trade union fees, deducted from pay		£55
payments total		**£6,325**

The four amounts, shown in the right-hand column on the previous page, are recorded in the journal and entered into the general ledger accounts. This is done as follows:

Step 1

Transfer the total of the payments (here £6,325) to wages account (this is the cost to the employer) and to wages control account.

Journal

Date	Details	Reference	Dr	Cr
20-8			£	£
30 Nov	Wages expense	GL	6,325	
	Wages control	GL		6,325
	Transfer of wages expense			

Dr		**Wages Expense Account**		Cr
20-8		£	20-8	£
30 Nov	Wages control	6,325		

Dr		**Wages Control Account**		Cr
20-8		£	20-8	£
			30 Nov Wages expense	6,325

Note: this total agrees with the payments total of £6,325 (shown on the previous page) which is the total payroll expense to the business for the month.

Step 2

Make entries for the payment of wages (the net pay paid from the bank).

Journal

Date	Details	Reference	Dr	Cr
20-8			£	£
30 Nov	Wages control	GL	3,820	
	Bank	CB		3,820
	Net wages paid to employees			

Dr			Wages Control Account		Cr
20-8		£	20-8		£
30 Nov	Bank	3,820	30 Nov	Wages expense	6,325

Dr			Bank Account		Cr
20-8		£	20-8		£
			30 Nov	Wages control	3,820

Step 3

Transfer the amount due to HMRC to HM Revenue & Customs account.

Journal

Date	Details	Reference	Dr	Cr
20-8			£	£
30 Nov	Wages control	GL	1,900	
	HM Revenue & Customs	GL		1,900
	Amount due to HMRC			

The amount due is £1,900 and comprises income tax £900 and National Insurance contributions – employer's £550 and employees' £450.

Dr			Wages Control Account		Cr
20-8		£	20-8		£
30 Nov	Bank	3,820	30 Nov	Wages expense	6,325
30 Nov	HM Revenue & Customs	1,900			

Dr			HM Revenue & Customs Account		Cr
20-8		£	20-8		£
			30 Nov	Wages control	1,900

Note: This account shows HM Revenue & Customs as an other payable of the business. The liability will be paid by the business (*debit* HM Revenue & Customs, *credit* bank) during the next month.

Step 4
Transfer the amount due to the pension fund.

The amount due is £550 – employer's contribution £275, employee's contribution £275.

Journal

Date	Details	Reference	Dr	Cr
20-8			£	£
30 Nov	Wages control	GL	550	
	Pension fund	GL		550
	Amount due to pension fund			

Dr		**Wages Control Account**			Cr
20-8		£	20-8		£
30 Nov	Bank	3,820	30 Nov Wages expense	6,325	
30 Nov	HM Revenue & Customs	1,900			
30 Nov	Pension fund	550			

Dr	**Pension Fund Account**		Cr
20-8	£	20-8	£
		30 Nov Wages control	550

Note: This account shows the pension fund as an other payable of the business. The liability will be paid by the business (*debit* pension fund, *credit* bank) when payment is made to the pension fund provider during the next month.

Step 5
Transfer the amount due for voluntary deductions.

The amount due is £55, being the trade union fees.

Journal

Date	Details	Reference	Dr	Cr
20-8			£	£
30 Nov	Wages control	GL	55	
	Trade union fees	GL		55
	Amount due for trade union fees			

Dr			Wages Control Account		Cr
20-8		£	20-8		£
30 Nov	Bank	3,820	30 Nov Wages expense		6,325
30 Nov	HM Revenue & Customs	1,900			
30 Nov	Pension fund	550			
30 Nov	Trade union fees	55			
		6,325			6,325

Dr		Trade Union Fees Account		Cr
20-8		£	20-8	£
			30 Nov Wages control	55

Note: This account shows that trade union fees as an other payable of the business. The liability will be paid by the business (*debit* trade union fees, *credit* bank) when payment is made to the trade union during the next month.

conclusion

You will see from the journal and accounting entries shown above that the wages control account records all the payroll accounting transactions carried out each time the payroll is run. At the end of the process the control account balance reverts to zero – you will see above that the total of both sides after Step 5 transfer is £6,325 – ie the balance is nil.

MAKING JOURNAL ENTRIES

As we have seen in this chapter, the journal is the book of prime entry for non-regular transactions. Because of the irregular nature of journal transactions, it is important that they are correctly authorised by the appropriate person – such as the accounts supervisor, the administration manager, the owner of the business. The authorisation will, ideally, be a financial document – eg letter, email or other document – but may well be verbal – eg "write-off the account of Zelah Limited as an irrecoverable debt."

It is good practice to ensure that journal entries are checked by an appropriate person before they are entered into the double-entry bookkeeping system. It is all too easy to get a journal entry the wrong way round resulting in an error.

In the next chapter we will look at the use of the journal when correcting errors in the accounting system.

Chapter Summary

- The journal is maintained in order to record non-regular transactions.

- The journal is a book of prime entry – it is not a double-entry account.

- Journal entries are prepared from authorised financial documents, which are stored securely for possible future reference.

- The journal records:
  - opening entries
  - irrecoverable debts written off
  - payroll transactions
  - correction of errors (see Chapter 8)

- Payroll transactions require journal and accounting entries for:
  - gross pay
  - net pay
  - income tax
  - employer's and employees' National Insurance contributions
  - employer's and employees' pension contributions
  - voluntary deductions from employees' pay

Key Terms

journal	the book of prime entry for non-regular transactions
opening entries	the transactions to open the accounts of a new business
irrecoverable debt	a debt owing to a business which it considers will never be paid
payroll transactions	the accounting entries which record wages and salaries paid to employees
wages control account	the main account for payroll through which all transactions for payroll pass
gross pay	the amount of employees' pay before any deductions
net pay	the amount paid to employees after deductions for income tax, employees' National Insurance contributions, employees' pension fund contributions, and voluntary deductions
HM Revenue & Customs	receives amounts from payroll in respect of income tax, employer's National Insurance contributions, and employees' National Insurance contribution

Activities

7.1 Hussain Limited is a furniture manufacturer. Which one of the following transactions will be recorded in the journal?

(a) sale of furniture on credit to a customer

(b) cash purchase of fabric for chair seat covers

(c) write off of a trade receivable's account from sales ledger as an irrecoverable debt

(d) petty cash purchase of postage stamps

Answer (a) or (b) or (c) or (d)

7.2 Which one of the following will not be recorded in the journal?

(a) payroll transactions

(b) cash sale of goods

(c) write off of an irrecoverable debt

(d) opening entries

Answer (a) or (b) or (c) or (d)

7.3 Which financial transaction goes with which book of prime entry?

financial transaction	book of prime entry
• opening entries for a new business	• petty cash book
• credit purchase of goods from a supplier	• sales day book
• returned credit purchases to the supplier	• purchases day book
• customer returns goods sold on credit	• sales returns day book
• BACS receipt from a customer	• purchases returns day book
• credit sale of goods to a customer	• journal
• expense paid out of petty cash	• cash book

7.4 Lucy Wallis started in business on 1 May 20-8 with the following assets and liabilities:

	£
Vehicle	6,500
Fixtures and fittings	2,800
Inventory	4,100
Bank	150
Loan from husband	5,000

You are to prepare Lucy's opening journal entry, showing clearly her capital at 1 May 20-8.

7.5   Jane Seymour is setting up a new business and has listed all the accounts and their amounts that will be used. She asks you to complete the journal entry by ticking the appropriate column in the table below, and to calculate her opening capital.

Account name	Amount £	Debit ✔	Credit ✔
Cash	200		
Cash at bank	2,340		
Capital			
Trade payables	3,985		
Trade receivables	4,751		
Loan from bank	12,650		
Office equipment	4,120		
Rent paid	950		
Inventory	2,310		
Sundry expenses	1,194		
Vehicles	8,350		
Wages	2,294		

7.6   You are an accounts assistant at Baxter Limited. The accounts supervisor has sent you an email instructing you to write off as an irrecoverable debt the account of Boughton and Company, a trade receivable who owes £240 plus VAT at 20%. Which one of the following sets of transactions will you make in the general ledger?

(a)   debit irrecoverable debts £288; credit VAT £48; credit sales ledger control £240

(b)   debit sales ledger control £288; credit irrecoverable debts £288

(c)   debit irrecoverable debts £240; debit VAT £48; credit bank £288

(d)   debit irrecoverable debts £240; debit VAT £48; credit sales ledger control £288

Answer (a) or (b) or (c) or (d)

7.7 You are employed by Tyax Trading as an accounts assistant. Today the accounts supervisor sends you the following email:

EMAIL

To	accountsassistant@tyax.co.uk
From	accountssupervisor@tyax.co.uk
Subject	Sales Ledger: Smithers and Sons

The above credit customer has ceased trading, owing us £840 plus VAT at 20%. Please record the journal entries needed in general ledger to write off as an irrecoverable debt the net amount and the VAT. Use the layout below.

Account name	Amount £	Debit ✔	Credit ✔

The following information is used in multiple-choice questions 7.8 to 7.10. In each case, choose one option from (a) to (d)

The payroll system of Home Fires Limited has recorded the following totals for the month of July:

gross pay	£350,780
income tax	£69,500
employer's National Insurance contributions	£35,085
employees' National Insurance contributions	£31,450
employer's pension contributions	£7,500
employees' pension contributions	£7,500
trade union fees	£1,500

7.8 The total payment to the HM Revenue & Customs for the month is:

(a) £100,950

(b) £104,585

(c) £15,000

(d) £136,035

7.9 The total wages expense to the employer is:

(a) £350,780

(b) £462,865

(c) £393,365

(d) £308,195

7.10 The total net pay to employees is:

(a) £240,830

(b) £248,330

(c) £388,230

(d) £349,280

7.11 Pegasus Limited has recorded the following payroll totals for the month of October 20-3:

gross pay	£101,500
income tax	£20,500
employer's National Insurance contributions	£10,150
employees' National Insurance contributions	£9,860
trade union fees	£850

You are to:

(a) Calculate the total payroll cost to the employer

(b) Calculate the payment due to HM Revenue & Customs

(c) Calculate the net pay due to employees

(d) Prepare journals dated 31 October 20-3 to show the entries needed in general ledger to record:

- the wages expense
- the liability to HM Revenue & Customs
- the net wages paid to employees
- the liability for trade union fees

7.12 Jason's Wool Shop has recorded the following payroll totals for the month of January 20-5:

gross pay	£50,000
income tax	£11,110
employer's National Insurance contributions	£5,010
employees' National Insurance contributions	£4,985
employer's pension contributions	£1,100
employees' pension contributions	£1,100

Jason's Wool Shop uses the following general ledger accounts for payroll transactions: wages control, wages expense, bank, HM Revenue & Customs, and pension fund.

You are to:

Use the journals below to show the entries needed in general ledger to:

(a)   record the wages expense

(b)   record the liability to HM Revenue & Customs

(c)   record the net wages paid to the employees

(d)   record the liability to the pension fund

(a)

Account name	Amount £	Debit ✔	Credit ✔

(b)

Account name	Amount £	Debit ✔	Credit ✔

(c)

Account name	Amount £	Debit ✔	Credit ✔

(d)

Account name	Amount £	Debit ✔	Credit ✔

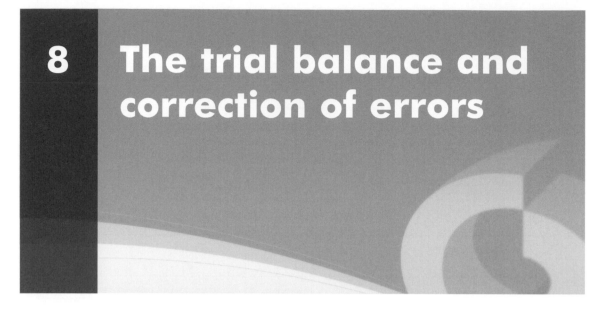

8 The trial balance and correction of errors

this chapter covers...

The trial balance lists the balances of every account from the ledger, distinguishing between those accounts which have debit balances and those which have credit balances.

The debit balances and credit balances are totalled and, when the two totals are the same, this proves that the accounting records are arithmetically correct. The initial trial balance has been covered in the unit for Processing Bookkeeping Transactions.

A trial balance does not prove the complete accuracy of the accounting records and there may well be errors. These fall into two groups:

- *errors not disclosed by the trial balance*
- *errors disclosed by the trial balance*

In this chapter, we look at the types of errors within each of these groups and, when they are found, we explain how to correct them using journal entries and see how the trial balance is redrafted following adjustments.

EXTRACTING A TRIAL BALANCE

An initial trial balance is extracted from the accounting records in order to make an initial check of the arithmetical accuracy of the double-entry bookkeeping, ie that the debit entries equal the credit entries.

A trial balance is a list of the balances of every account from general ledger (including cash book and petty cash book), distinguishing between those accounts which have debit balances and those which have credit balances.

A trial balance is extracted at regular intervals – often at the end of each month – and the balances are set out in two totalled columns, a debit column and a credit column. The debit and credit columns are totalled and the totals should agree. In this way the trial balance proves that the accounting records are arithmetically correct. However, a trial balance does not prove the complete accuracy of the accounting records as there may well be errors – which we will look at in this chapter.

An example of a trial balance is shown below.

Trial balance of Ace Suppliers as at 31 January 20-4	Dr £	Cr £
Name of account		
Purchases	7,500	
Sales		16,000
Sales returns	250	
Purchases returns		500
Sales ledger control	1,550	
Purchases ledger control		900
Rent	1,000	
Wages	1,500	
Heating and lighting	1,250	
Office equipment	5,000	
Machinery	7,500	
Inventory at 1 Jan 20-4	2,500	
Petty cash	200	
Bank (cash at bank)	4,850	
Value Added Tax		1,200
J Williams: loan		7,000
Capital		10,000
Drawings	2,500	
	35,600	35,600

Note that the order of accounts in the trial balance could be set out:

– in alphabetical order, or

– in random order (as on the previous page), or

– in the order of final accounts, that is income and expenditure items from the income statement, followed by asset, liability and capital items from the statement of financial position

ERRORS IN THE ACCOUNTING SYSTEM

In any accounting system there is always the possibility of errors. As noted in the previous section, a trial balance does not prove the complete accuracy of the accounting records and there may well be errors.

Ways to avoid errors, or ways to reveal them sooner, include:

■ division of the accounting function between a number of people, so that no one person is responsible for all aspects of a business transaction

■ regular circulation of statements of account to customers, who will check the transactions on their accounts and advise any discrepancies

■ checking of statements of account received from suppliers against the accounting records

■ extraction of a trial balance at regular intervals

■ the checking of bank statements and preparing bank reconciliation statements

■ checking cash and petty cash balances against cash held

■ the use of control accounts

■ the use of a computer accounting program

Despite all of these precautions, errors will still occur from time-to-time.

We will look at:

■ correction of errors not shown by a trial balance

■ correction of errors shown by a trial balance, using a suspense account

We will look at each of these two groups and will see the journal entry needed to correct the various types of errors, together with the ledger entries and the effect on the trial balance.

ERRORS NOT DISCLOSED BY THE TRIAL BALANCE

As mentioned earlier, a trial balance does not prove the complete accuracy of the accounting records.

There are six types of errors that are not disclosed by the trial balance, as follows:

error of omission

Here a financial transaction has been completely omitted from the accounting records, ie both the debit and credit entries have not been made.

error of commission

Here, a transaction is entered to the wrong person's account. For example, a sale of goods on credit to T Hughes has been entered as debit to J Hughes' account. Double-entry bookkeeping has been completed and the sales ledger control account will reconcile with the sales ledger. However, when J Hughes receives a statement of account, he or she will soon complain about being debited with goods not ordered or received.

An error of commission can also occur between other accounts, such as expenses or non-current assets.

error of principle

This is when a transaction has been entered in the wrong type of account. For example, the cost of fuel for vehicles has been entered as debit vehicles account, credit bank account. The error is that vehicles account is a non-current asset, and the transaction should have been debited to the expense account for vehicle running expenses. If not corrected such an error of principle will show a false financial position for the business.

error of original entry

Here, the correct accounts have been used, and the correct sides: what is wrong is that the amount has been entered incorrectly in both accounts. This could be caused by a 'bad figure' on an invoice or a cheque, or it could be caused by a 'reversal of figures', eg an amount of £45 being entered in both accounts as £54. Note that both debit and credit entries need to be made incorrectly for the trial balance still to balance; if one entry has been made incorrectly and the other is correct, then the error will be shown.

reversal of entries

With this error, the debit and credit entries have been made in the accounts but on the wrong side of the two accounts concerned. For example, a cash sale has been entered wrongly as debit sales account, credit cash account. (This should be entered as debit cash account, credit sales account.)

compensating error

Here two errors cancel each other out. For example, if the balance of purchases account is calculated wrongly at £10 too much, and a similar error has occurred in calculating the balance of sales account, then the two errors will compensate each other, and the trial balance will not show the errors.

Although these errors are not shown by a trial balance, they are likely to come to light if the procedures suggested on the previous page, are followed. For example, a customer will soon let you know if their account has been debited with goods they did not buy.

When an error is found, it needs to be corrected by means of a journal entry which shows the correcting bookkeeping entries. Remember that all journal entries are prepared from authorised financial documents – these could take the form of an email or a note from the accounts supervisor; such documents, together with any other paperwork, should be stored securely for possible future reference.

We will now look at an example of each of the errors not shown by a trial balance, and will see how it is corrected by means of a journal entry.

A practical hint which may help in correcting errors is to write out the double-entry accounts as they appear with the error; then write in the correcting entries and see if the result has achieved what was intended.

ERRORS NOT DISCLOSED BY THE TRIAL BALANCE: JOURNAL ENTRIES

We will now discuss the errors which are not disclosed by the trial balance and see an example journal entry for each. Remember that:

- the journal is the book of prime entry for non-regular transactions
- journal entries must be recorded in the accounting system
- for journal entries which involve sales ledger control account or purchases ledger control account, the transactions must also be recorded in the accounts in the subsidiary ledger – either sales ledger or purchases ledger

For each example error, the correcting journal and ledger entries are shown.

error of omission

Credit sale of goods, £200 plus VAT (at 20%) on invoice 4967 to H Jarvis completely omitted from the accounting system; the error is corrected on 12 May 20-4.

Date	Details	Reference	Dr	Cr
20-4			£	£
12 May	Sales ledger control	GL	240	
	Sales	GL		200
	VAT	GL		40
			240	240
	Invoice 4967 omitted from accounts: in the sales ledger – debit H Jarvis £240			

GENERAL LEDGER

Dr   **Sales Ledger Control Account**   Cr

20-4		£	20-4		£
12 May	Sales/VAT	240			

Dr   **Sales Account**   Cr

20-4		£	20-4		£
			12 May	Sales ledger control	200

Dr   **Value Added Tax Account**   Cr

20-4		£	20-4		£
			12 May	Sales ledger control	40

SALES LEDGER

Dr   **H Jarvis**   Cr

20-4		£	20-4		£
12 May	Sales/VAT	240			

An error of omission can happen in a very small business – often where the bookkeeping is done by one person: for example, an invoice is 'lost' down the back of a filing cabinet. Where a computer accounting system is used, it should be impossible for this error to occur. Also, if documents are numbered in sequence, then none should be mislaid.

error of commission

Credit sales of £48, including VAT (at 20%) on invoice no 321 have been debited to the account of J Adams, instead of the account of J Adams Limited; the error is corrected on 17 May 20-4.

Date	Details	Reference	Dr	Cr
20-4			£	£
17 May	Sales ledger control	GL	48	
	Sales ledger control	GL		48
	Correction of error (invoice 321):			
	in the sales ledger			
	– debit J Adams Limited £48			
	– credit J Adams £48			

GENERAL LEDGER

Dr	**Sales Ledger Control Account**			Cr
20-4		£	20-4	£
17 May	Sales ledger control	48	17 May Sales ledger control	48

SALES LEDGER

Dr	**J Adams Limited**			Cr
20-4		£	20-4	£
17 May	J Adams	48		

Dr	**J Adams**			Cr
20-4		£	20-4	£
			17 May J Adams Limited	48

An error of commission can be avoided, to some extent, by the use of account numbers, and by persuading the customer to quote the account number or reference on each transaction. All computer accounting systems use numbers/references to identify accounts, but it is still possible to post a transaction to the wrong account.

An error of commission can also occur between other accounts, such as expenses or non-current assets. For example, if an expense for advertising has been debited in error to administrative expenses account, this will need to be corrected through a journal entry and the two accounts involved.

error of principle

The cost of diesel fuel, £50 (excluding VAT) on receipt no 34535, has been debited to vehicles account; the error is corrected on 20 May 20-4.

Date	Details	Reference	Dr	Cr
20-4			£	£
20 May	Vehicle expenses	GL	50	
	Vehicles	GL		50
	Correction of error: receipt 34535			

GENERAL LEDGER

Dr	**Vehicle Expenses Account**			Cr
20-4		£	20-4	£
20 May	Vehicles	50		

Dr	**Vehicles Account**		Cr
20-4	£	20-4	£
		20 May Vehicle expenses	50

An error of principle is similar to an error of commission except that, instead of the wrong person's account being used, it is the wrong class of account.

In the above example, the vehicle running costs must be kept separate from the cost of the asset (the vehicle), otherwise the expense and asset accounts will be incorrect, leading to the ledger accounts showing a false financial position for the business.

error of original entry

Postages of £45 paid by cheque entered in the accounts as £54; the error is corrected on 27 May 20-4.

Do not correct an error like this by putting an amount for the difference through the accounts – here by debiting bank and crediting postages with £9. The reason for saying this is that there was no original transaction for this amount. Instead we must make two journal entries to:

■ remove the incorrect entry

■ record the correct entry

In this example, the journal entries are:

Date	Details	Reference	Dr	Cr
20-4			£	£
27 May	Bank	CB	54	
	Postages	GL		54
	Removing the incorrect entry:			
	transaction entered as £54			
	instead of £45			

Date	Details	Reference	Dr	Cr
20-4			£	£
27 May	Postages	GL	45	
	Bank	CB		45
	Recording the correct entry:			
	transaction entered as £54			
	instead of £45			

GENERAL LEDGER

Dr		**Cash Book** (bank columns)		Cr
20-4	£	20-4		£
27 May Postages	54	27 May Postages		45

Dr		**Postages Account**		Cr
20-4	£	20-4		£
27 May Bank	45	27 May Bank		54

A reversal of figures either has a difference of nine (as above), or an amount divisible by nine. An error of original entry can also be a 'bad' figure on a cheque or an invoice, entered wrongly into both accounts.

reversal of entries

A payment, on 3 May 20-4 by cheque for £50 to a trade payable, S Wright (cheque no 093459), has been debited in the cash book and credited to purchases ledger control account; this is corrected on 12 May 20-4.

This error is corrected by two journal entries. Although the error here could be corrected by debiting purchases ledger control account and crediting bank with £100, there was no original transaction for this amount. Instead we must make two journal entries to:

■ remove the incorrect entry

■ record the correct entry

In this example the journal entries are:

Date	Details	Reference	Dr	Cr
20-4			£	£
12 May	Purchases ledger control	GL	50	
	Bank	CB		50
	Removing the incorrect entry			
	(cheque no 093459):			
	in the purchases ledger debit			
	S Wright £50			

Date	Details	Reference	Dr	Cr
20-4			£	£
12 May	Purchases ledger control	GL	50	
	Bank	CB		50
	Recording the correct entry			
	(cheque no 093459):			
	in the purchases ledger debit			
	S Wright £50			

It is often an idea to write out the accounts, complete with the error, and then to write in the correcting entries. The two accounts involved in this last error are shown with the error made on 3 May, and the corrections made on 12 May indicated by the shading:

GENERAL LEDGER

Dr			**Purchases Ledger Control Account**			Cr
20-4		£	20-4			£
12 May	Bank	50	3 May	Bank		50
12 May	Bank	50				

Dr			**Cash Book** (bank columns)			Cr
20-4		£	20-4			£
3 May	S Wright	50	12 May	S Wright		50
			12 May	S Wright		50

The accounts now show a net debit transaction of £50 on purchases ledger control account, and a net credit transaction of £50 on bank account, which is how this payment to a supplier should have been recorded in the first place.

compensating error

Rent account is overcast (ie it is over-added) by £100; sales account is also overcast by the same amount; the error is corrected on 31 May 20-4.

Date	Details	Reference	Dr	Cr
20-4			£	£
31 May	Sales	GL	100	
	Rent	GL		100
	Correction of overcast on rent			
	account and sales account			

GENERAL LEDGER

Dr			Sales Account		Cr
20-4		£	20-4		£
31 May	Rent	100			

Dr			Rent Account		Cr
20-4		£	20-4		£
			31 May	Sales	100

In this example, an account with a debit balance – rent – has been overcast; this is compensated by an overcast on an account with a credit balance – sales. There are several permutations on this theme, eg two debit balances, one overcast, one undercast; a debit balance undercast, a credit balance undercast.

TRIAL BALANCE ERRORS: USE OF SUSPENSE ACCOUNT

There are six types of errors which are disclosed by the trial balance:
- calculation errors in ledger accounts
- single entry transactions
- recording two debits or two credits for a transaction
- recording different amounts for the debit and credit entries
- errors in transferring balances to the trial balance
- omission of a general ledger account in the trial balance

When errors are disclosed, the initial trial balance is 'balanced' by creating a journal entry for the difference and opening a suspense account, as shown in the Case Study below.

Case Study

SUSPENSE ACCOUNT

situation

The accounts assistant of Temeside Traders is unable to balance the initial trial balance on 31 December 20-4. As the error or errors cannot be found quickly, the trial balance is balanced by creating a journal entry for the difference and opening a suspense account:

	Dr	Cr
	£	£
Trial balance totals	100,000	99,700
Suspense account		300
	100,000	100,000

solution

A journal entry is created to open a suspense account with, in this case, a credit balance of £300:

Date	Details	Reference	Dr	Cr
20-4 31 Dec	Suspense *Trial balance difference as at* *31 December 20-4*	GL	£	£ 300

The suspense account is opened in general ledger as follows:

GENERAL LEDGER

Dr		Suspense Account		Cr
20-4		£	20-4	£
			31 Dec Trial balance difference	300

A detailed examination of the bookkeeping system is now made in order to find the errors. As errors are found, they are corrected by means of a journal entry. The journal entries will balance, with one part of the entry being either a debit or credit to suspense account. In this way, the balance on suspense account will be eliminated by bookkeeping transactions.

In the next section we will discuss how errors which are disclosed by the trial balance are corrected and will see an example journal entry for each.

ERRORS DISCLOSED BY THE TRIAL BALANCE: JOURNAL ENTRIES

We will now look at the journal entries needed to correct errors which are disclosed by the trial balance and present an example for each.

At the end of this section we will see how the suspense account from the Case Study above appears after the errors have been found and corrected on 4 January 20-5.

calculation errors in ledger accounts

Sales account was undercast (under-added) by £100 on 23 December 20-4.

As sales account was undercast, the correcting entry must credit sales account with £100. The correcting journal entry and ledger entry are:

Date	Details	Reference	Dr	Cr
20-5			£	£
4 Jan	Suspense	GL	100	
	Sales	GL		100
	Undercast on 23 December 20-4			
	now corrected			

GENERAL LEDGER

Dr		Sales Account		Cr
20-5	£	20-5		£
		4 Jan	Suspense	100

The entry in suspense account is shown on page 164.

single entry transactions

Telephone expenses of £55 were not recorded in the expenses account on 10 December 20-4.

As only the bank entry has been recorded, the correcting entry must complete double-entry bookkeeping by debiting telephone expenses account with £55. The correcting journal entry and ledger entry are:

Date	Details	Reference	Dr	Cr
20-5			£	£
4 Jan	Telephone expenses	GL	55	
	Suspense	GL		55
	Omission of entry in expenses			
	account: paid from bank			
	on 10 December 20-4			

GENERAL LEDGER

Dr		Telephone Expenses Account		Cr
20-5	£	20-5		£
4 Jan	Suspense	55		

The entry in suspense account is shown on page 164.

recording two debits or two credits for a transaction

Stationery expenses of £48 were debited to both stationery account and bank account on 18 December 20-4.

As bank account has been debited in error with £48, the correcting journal entry must be in two parts to:

■ remove the incorrect entry

■ record the correct entry

Date	Details	Reference	Dr	Cr
20-5			£	£
4 Jan	Suspense	GL	48	
	Bank	CB		48
	Removing the incorrect entry: payment for stationery expenses debited to bank in error on 18 December 20-4			

Date	Details	Reference	Dr	Cr
20-5			£	£
4 Jan	Suspense	GL	48	
	Bank	CB		48
	Recording the correct entry: payment for stationery expenses debited to bank in error on 18 December 20-4			

GENERAL LEDGER

Dr		**Cash Book** (bank columns)		Cr
20-5	£	20-5		£
		4 Jan	Suspense	48
		4 Jan	Suspense	48

The entries in suspense account are shown on page 164.

recording different amounts for debit and credit entries

Payment made to A Wilson, a supplier, for £65 has been entered in bank account as £56 on 19 December 20-4.

As the credit entry in bank account has been entered incorrectly, the correcting journal entry must be in two parts to:

■ remove the incorrect entry

■ record the correct entry

Date	Details	Reference	Dr	Cr
20-5			£	£
4 Jan	Bank	CB	56	
	Suspense	GL		56
	Removing the incorrect entry:			
	payment to a supplier entered in			
	bank account as £56 instead of			
	£65 on 19 December 20-4			

Date	Details	Reference	Dr	Cr
20-5			£	£
4 Jan	Suspense	GL	65	
	Bank	CB		65
	Recording the correct entry:			
	payment to a supplier entered in			
	bank account as £56 instead of			
	£65 on 19 December 20-4			

GENERAL LEDGER

Dr			**Cash Book** (bank columns)		Cr
20-5		£	20-5		£
4 Jan	Suspense	56	4 Jan	Suspense	65

The entries in suspense account are shown on page 164.

errors in transferring balances to the trial balance

The balance of rent account is £11,100 but it has been recorded in the trial balance as £11,000.

To correct this type of error needs a journal entry to take the wrong amount from suspense account and then to record the correct amount, ie a two-part journal entry. As rent account has a debit balance the journal entries are firstly to take out the wrong balance (debit suspense account and credit rent account in the trial balance) and then to record the correct balance (debit rent account in the trial balance and credit suspense account).

Date	Details	Reference	Dr	Cr
20-5			£	£
4 Jan	Suspense	GL	11,000	
	Removing the incorrect balance of rent account from the trial balance as at 31 December 20-4			

Date	Details	Reference	Dr	Cr
20-5			£	£
4 Jan	Suspense	GL		11,100
	Recording the correct balance of rent account in the trial balance as at 31 December 20-4			

Each of these journal entries is for a single transaction; the reason for this is because the account for rent is correct in general ledger and is not affected by the error of recording the wrong amount in the trial balance.

The entries in suspense account are shown on page 164.

Note that some businesses may have a policy of not recording journal entries to correct this type of error. As the ledger account balance is correct, policy might be to amend the incorrect balance and the balance of suspense account directly on the face of the trial balance.

omission of a general ledger account in the trial balance

Discount received account has been omitted from the trial balance. The balance of the account is £250 credit.

To correct this type of error needs a journal entry to record the balance which has been omitted. As this example omits an account with a credit balance we must record the inclusion of the account as debit suspense account and credit discount received account in the trial balance.

Date	Details	Reference	Dr	Cr
20-5			£	£
4 Jan	Suspense	GL	250	
	Recording the correct balance of discount received account in the trial balance as at 31 December 20-4			

This is a single entry transaction in the journal because the omitted account is correct in general ledger and is not affected by its omission in the trial balance. The entry in suspense account is shown below.

Note that some businesses may have a policy of correcting this type of error directly on the face of the trial balance without recording a journal entry.

suspense account

After these journal entries have been recorded in the general ledger accounts, suspense account appears as:

Dr			**Suspense Account**			Cr
20-5		£	20-4			£
4 Jan	Sales	100	31 Dec	Trial balance difference		300
4 Jan	Bank	48	20-5			
4 Jan	Bank	48	4 Jan	Telephone expenses		55
4 Jan	Bank	65	4 Jan	Bank		56
4 Jan	Rent	11,000	4 Jan	Rent		11,100
4 Jan	Discount received	250				
		11,511				11,511

Thus all the errors have been found, and suspense account now has a nil balance.

REDRAFT THE TRIAL BALANCE FOLLOWING ADJUSTMENTS

In the previous section we have seen how a suspense account is used to 'balance' an initial trial balance. The suspense account can have either a debit or a credit balance – it will depend on which of the columns of the initial trial balance is the lower amount. For example, from the Case Study on pages 206-207, the credit column of the trial balance was £300 less than the debit column: this means that £300 had to be credited to suspense account to 'balance' the trial balance.

Once a suspense account has been opened it is necessary to locate the errors in the accounting system – we have seen the six types of error that are revealed by a trial balance. When they have been found, the errors will be corrected by means of journal entries from which the ledgers will be updated. Correcting errors will have an effect on the trial balance and it is necessary to redraft the trial balance in order to show:

- that suspense account has been cleared
- the adjusted account balances

The Case Study which follows shows how an initial trial balance is redrafted to clear suspense account and adjust the account balances.

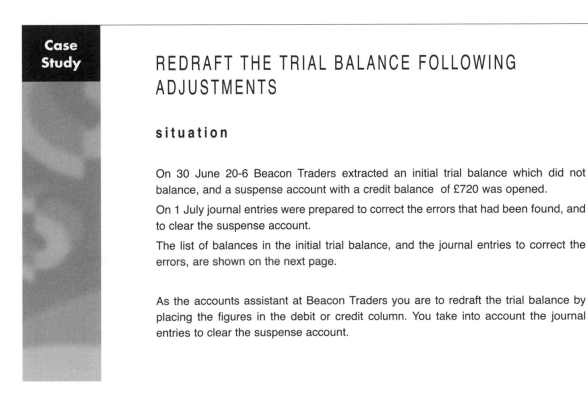

Case Study

REDRAFT THE TRIAL BALANCE FOLLOWING ADJUSTMENTS

situation

On 30 June 20-6 Beacon Traders extracted an initial trial balance which did not balance, and a suspense account with a credit balance of £720 was opened.

On 1 July journal entries were prepared to correct the errors that had been found, and to clear the suspense account.

The list of balances in the initial trial balance, and the journal entries to correct the errors, are shown on the next page.

As the accounts assistant at Beacon Traders you are to redraft the trial balance by placing the figures in the debit or credit column. You take into account the journal entries to clear the suspense account.

Account name	Balances extracted on 30 June 20-6	Balances at 1 July 20-6	
	£	Debit £	Credit £
Vehicles	20,500		
Inventory	11,945		
Bank (overdraft)	7,847		
Petty cash control	110		
Sales ledger control	28,368		
Purchases ledger control	12,591		
VAT owing to HM Revenue & Customs	2,084		
Capital	20,670		
Loan from bank	20,500		
Sales	84,567		
Sales returns	1,089		
Purchases	51,054		
Purchases returns	2,210		
Vehicle expenses	3,175		
Wages	22,864		
Rent and rates	8,210		
Advertising	2,174		
Heating and lighting	968		
Telephone	732		
Suspense account (credit balance)	720		
	Totals		

Journal entries

Account name	Debit £	Credit £
Suspense	225	
Bank		225
Suspense	225	
Bank		225

Account name	Debit £	Credit £
Sales	4,250	
Suspense		4,250
Suspense	4,520	
Sales		4,520

solution

The first thing you do is to check that the journal entries will clear the suspense account. You do this by writing up the suspense account from the journal entries as follows:

Dr		Suspense Account			Cr
20-6		£	20-6		£
1 Jul	Bank	225	30 Jun	Trial balance difference	720
1 Jul	Bank	225	1 Jul	Sales	4,250
1 Jul	Sales	4,520			
		4,970			4,970

Next you amend the account balances affected by the journal entries:

Dr		Bank Account			Cr
20-6		£	20-6		£
1 Jul	Balance c/d	8,297	30 Jun	Balance b/d	7,847
			1 Jul	Suspense	225
			1 Jul	Suspense	225
		8,297			8,297
			1 Jul	Balance b/d	8,297

Dr		Sales Account			Cr
20-6		£	20-6		£
1 Jul	Suspense	4,250	30 Jun	Balance b/d	84,567
1 Jul	Balance c/d	84,837	1 Jul	Suspense	4,520
		89,087			89,087
			1 Jul	Balance b/d	84,837

Lastly you redraft the trial balance, on the next page, which balances without using a suspense account. This shows that the accounting records are now arithmetically correct.

Account name	Balances extracted on 30 June 20-6	Balances at 1 July 20-6	
	£	Debit £	Credit £
Vehicles	20,500	20,500	
Inventory	11,945	11,945	
Bank (overdraft)	7,847		8,297
Petty cash control	110	110	
Sales ledger control	28,368	28,368	
Purchases ledger control	12,591		12,591
VAT owing to HM Revenue & Customs	2,084		2,084
Capital	20,670		20,670
Loan from bank	20,500		20,500
Sales	84,567		84,837
Sales returns	1,089	1,089	
Purchases	51,054	51,054	
Purchases returns	2,210		2,210
Vehicle expenses	3,175	3,175	
Wages	22,864	22,864	
Rent and rates	8,210	8,210	
Advertising	2,174	2,174	
Heating and lighting	968	968	
Telephone	732	732	
Suspense account			–
Totals		151,189	151,189

Tutorial note: the accounts affected by the journal entries are bank, sales and suspense.

Chapter Summary	

■   Taking the balance of each account in general ledger, a trial balance can be extracted.

■   A trial balance does not prove the complete accuracy of the accounting records as there may be:
  – errors not disclosed by the trial balance
  – errors disclosed by the trial balance

■   Errors not disclosed by the trial balance are:
  – error of omission
  – error of commission
  – error of principle
  – error of original entry
  – reversal of entries
  – compensating error

■   Errors disclosed by the trial balance are:
  – calculation errors in ledger accounts
  – single entry transactions
  – recording two debits or two credits for a transaction
  – recording different amounts for the debit and credit entries
  – errors in transferring balances to the trial balance
  – omission of a general ledger account in the trial balance

■   Correction of errors is always a difficult topic to put into practice: it tests knowledge of double-entry bookkeeping and it is all too easy to make the error worse than it was in the first place! The secret of correcting errors is to write down – in account format – what has gone wrong. It should then be relatively easy to see what has to be done to put the error right.

■   All errors are non-regular transactions and need to be corrected by means of a journal entry: the bookkeeper then records the correcting transactions in the accounts.

■   When error(s) are disclosed by the trial balance, the amount of the error is placed in a suspense account. As the errors are found, journal entries are made which 'clear out' the suspense account.

Key Terms		
	trial balance	list of the balances of every account from general ledger (including cash book and petty cash book), distinguishing between those accounts which have debit balances and those which have credit balances
	error of omission	financial transaction completely omitted from the accounting records
	error of commission	transaction entered to the wrong person's account, or between other accounts, such as expenses or non-current assets
	error of principle	transaction entered in the wrong type of account
	error of original entry	wrong amount entered incorrectly in accounts
	reversal of entries	debit and credit entries made on the wrong side of the accounts
	compensating error	where two errors cancel each other
	suspense account	account in which is placed the amount of an error shown by the initial trial balance, pending further investigation
	redrafted trial balance	trial balance which has been amended following correction of errors

Activities

8.1 The following errors have been made in the accounting records of Beacon Traders. Tick to show which of the errors below are, or are not, disclosed by the trial balance.

Error in the general ledger	Error disclosed by the trial balance	Error not disclosed by the trial balance
A bank payment for telephone expenses has been recorded on the debit side of both the cash book and telephone expenses account		
A payment recorded in bank account for vehicle repairs has been entered in vehicles account		
A sales invoice has been omitted from all accounting records		
The balance of purchases returns account has been calculated incorrectly		
A bank payment from a trade receivable has been recorded in cash book and sales ledger only		
A bank payment of £85 for stationery has been recorded as £58 in both accounts		

8.2 An amount has been entered into the accounting system as £65 instead of £56. The error is called:

(a)   compensating error

(b)   error of commission

(c)   error of principle

(d)   error of original entry

Which one of these options is correct?

8.3 A trial balance failed to balance. The debit column totalled £154,896 and the credit column totalled £155,279. What entry would be made in the suspense account to balance the trial balance?

(a) £766 debit

(b) £383 debit

(c) £383 credit

(d) £766 credit

8.4 A trial balance fails to agree by £75 and the difference is placed in a suspense account. Later it is found that a cash sale for this amount has not been entered in the sales account. Which one of the following journal entries is correct?

(a) debit suspense account £75; credit sales account £75

(b) debit suspense account £150; credit sales account £150

(c) debit sales account £75; credit suspense account £75

(d) credit sales account £75

8.5 The following errors have been made in the general ledger of Mereford Manufacturing:

(a) £100 has been debited to rent account instead of to rates account.

(b) Sales returns have been entered into the accounting records as £96 instead of the correct amount of £69.

(c) Purchases returns of £175 have been debited to purchases returns account and credited to purchases ledger control account.

(d) Diesel fuel for vehicles of £45 has been debited to vehicles account.

You are to record the journal entries to correct the errors shown above in the general ledger (dates and narratives are not required).

8.6 The trial balance of Thomas Wilson balanced. However, a number of errors have been found in the accounting records:

(a) credit sale of £150 to J Rigby has not been entered in the accounts

(b) a bank payment for £125 to H Price Limited, a trade payable, has been recorded in the account of H Prince

(c) the cost of a new delivery van, £10,000, has been entered to vehicle expenses account

(d) postages of £55, paid by bank payment, have been entered on the wrong sides of both accounts

(e) both purchases account and purchases returns account have been undercast by £100

(f) a bank receipt for £89 from L Johnson, a trade receivable, has been entered in the accounts as £98

You are to take each error in turn and:

• state the type of error

• show the correcting journal entry

8.7 The trial balance of Rose's Retail included a suspense account. All the bookkeeping errors have now been traced and the journal entries shown below have been recorded.

Journal entries

Account name	Debit £	Credit £
Telephone expenses	210	
Suspense		210
Suspense	100	
Sales		100
Vehicle expenses	50	
Vehicles		50

As the accounts assistant at Rose's Retail, you are to post the journal entries to the general ledger accounts. Dates are not required.

Telephone Expenses Account

Details	Amount £	Details	Amount £

Suspense Account

Details	Amount £	Details	Amount £
Balance b/d	110		

Sales Account

Details	Amount £	Details	Amount £

Vehicle Expenses Account

Details	Amount £	Details	Amount £

Vehicles Account

Details	Amount £	Details	Amount £

8.8 (a) The initial trial balance of Carrick Cards at 30 April 20-1 did not balance. The difference of £100 was placed into a suspense account.

The error has been traced to the sales day book as shown below.

Sales day book

Date 20-1	Details	Invoice number	Total £	VAT £	Net £
30 Apr	Bialas Ltd	4591	2,400	400	2,000
30 Apr	Corline and Co	4592	1,440	240	1,200
30 Apr	Thorpe Traders	4593	960	160	800
	Totals		4,800	700	4,000

As an accounts assistant at Carrick Cards you are to identify the error and record the journal entries needed for the general ledger to:

(i) remove the incorrect entry

(ii) record the correct entry

(iii) remove the suspense account balance

(i)

Account name	Amount £	Debit ✔	Credit ✔

(ii)

Account name	Amount £	Debit ✔	Credit ✔

(iii)

Account name	Amount £	Debit ✔	Credit ✔

(b)   A further error is discovered – a bank payment for vehicle expenses of £89 has been entered in the accounts as £98.

You are to record the journal entries needed for the general ledger to:

(i)   remove the incorrect entry

(ii)   record the correct entry

(i)

Account name	Amount £	Debit ✔	Credit ✔

(ii)

Account name	Amount £	Debit ✔	Credit ✔

8.9   Jeremy Johnson extracts a trial balance from his accounting records on 30 September 20-4. Unfortunately the trial balance fails to balance and the difference, £19 debit, is placed to a suspense account pending further investigation.

The following errors are later found:

(a)   a bank payment of £85 for office expenses has been entered in the bank account but no entry has been made in the office expenses account

(b)   a bank payment for photocopying of £87 has been correctly entered in the bank account, but is shown as £78 in the photocopying account

(c)   sales returns account has been overcast by £100

(d)   commission received of £25 has been entered twice in the account

You are to:

·   make journal entries to correct the errors

·   show the suspense account after the errors have been corrected

8.10   On 31 December 20-4 Chapelporth Supplies extracted an initial trial balance which did not balance, and a suspense account was opened. On 2 January 20-5 journal entries were prepared to correct the errors that had been found, and to clear the suspense account. The list of balances in the initial trial balance, and the journal entries to correct the errors, are shown on the next page.

As the accounts assistant at Chapelporth Supplies you are to redraft the trial balance by placing the figures in the debit or credit column. You should take into account the journal entries which will clear the suspense account.

Account name	Balances extracted on 31 December 20-4	Balances at 2 January 20-5	
	£	Debit £	Credit £
Office equipment	12,246		
Bank (cash at bank)	3,091		
Petty cash control	84		
Inventory	11,310		
Capital	18,246		
Loan from bank	8,290		
VAT owing to HM Revenue & Customs	3,105		
Purchases ledger control	17,386		
Sales ledger control	30,274		
Sales	82,410		
Purchases	39,996		
Purchases returns	2,216		
Sales returns	3,471		
Wages	20,212		
Advertising	4,300		
Insurance	1,045		
Heating and lighting	1,237		
Rent and rates	4,076		
Postages	721		
Suspense account (credit balance)	410		
Totals			

Journal entries

Account name	Debit £	Credit £
Suspense	780	
Advertising		780
Advertising	870	
Suspense		870

Account name	Debit £	Credit £
Suspense	5,500	
Purchases		5,500
Purchases	5,000	
Suspense		5,000

8.11 On 30 April 20-8 Towanporth Traders extracted an initial trial balance which did not balance, and a suspense account was opened. On 1 May journal entries were prepared to correct the errors that had been found, and to clear the suspense account. The list of balances in the initial trial balance, and the journal entries to correct the errors, are shown below.

As the accounts assistant at Towanporth Traders, you are to redraft the trial balance by placing the figures in the debit or credit column. You should take into account the journal entries which will clear the suspense account.

Account name	Balances extracted on 30 April 20-8 £	Balances at 1 May 20-8	
		Debit £	Credit £
Sales	101,169		
Sales returns	3,476		
Purchases	54,822		
Purchases returns	4,107		
Sales ledger control	25,624		
Purchases ledger control	18,792		
Rent and rates	3,985		
Advertising	4,867		
Insurance	1,733		
Wages	27,391		
Heating and lighting	3,085		
Miscellaneous expenses	107		
Capital	18,171		
Vehicles	22,400		
Inventory	12,454		
Petty cash control	85		
Bank (overdraft)	6,041		
VAT owing to HM Revenue & Customs	3,054		
Loan from bank	12,200		
Suspense account (debit balance)	3,505		
Totals			

Journal entries

Account name	Debit £	Credit £
Suspense	100	
Sales		100

Account name	Debit £	Credit £
Wages	3,855	
Suspense		3,855

Account name	Debit £	Credit £
Suspense	125	
Bank		125
Suspense	125	
Bank		125

Answers to activities

CHAPTER 1: BANKS, BUILDING SOCIETIES AND PAYMENT SYSTEMS

1.1 (b)

1.2 Regular savings account, insurance, credit cards.

1.3 (c) and (f)

1.4 (b)

1.5 (a) 4, (b) 6, (c) 2.

1.6 False. The transaction will be refused if the money is not available.

1.7 (a)

1.8 (b)

1.9 (c)

1.10 (a)

1.11 (b)

1.12 (b)

1.13 (b)

1.14 (a) 6, (b) 1, (c) 3, (d) 4, (e) 2, (f) 5.

CHAPTER 2: MAKING PAYMENTS

2.1 False. No cheque is involved in a BACS payment.

2.2 For security reasons: to prevent fraudulent alterations.

2.3 To establish the legal relationship between the bank and the business. The bank has to know *who* can sign cheques, and for what amounts. It also needs specimen signatures so that it can verify written instructions, eg cheque signatures and other payment instructions.

2.4 (a) See text pages 64 and 67. (b) Standing order (c) Direct debit

2.5 (a) Bank draft (b) CHAPS

2.6 (a) He/she doesn't have to rely on carrying his/her own money; or he/she doesn't have to pay!

   (b) Monitoring of expenditure, or control of expenditure.

2.7 Note that the cash discount is not available – the period has expired. Total £15,255.34.

2.8 Total £4,083.05.

2.9 The most <u>normal</u> methods would be:
(a) BACS
(b) bank giro credit
(c) bank draft
(d) company credit card
(e) CHAPS

2.10 **standing order**

(a) Standing order completed as shown below.

(b) The form will be sent to the National Bank, as they will set up the payments.

(c) The standing order will have to be signed by an authorised signatory (or two) within the business. It should also be noted that details of the due payments will be passed to the person in charge of entering up the cash book as the payments will form part of the double-entry book-keeping of the company.

STANDING ORDER MANDATE

To ___NATIONAL___ Bank
Address ___10 CATHEDRAL STREET MEREFORD MR1 5DE___

PLEASE PAY TO

Bank ___BARCLAYS___ Branch ___EVESMORE___ Sort code ___30 98 15___
Beneficiary ___ Account number ___72627161___
The sum of £ ___350___ Amount in words ___THREE HUNDRED AND FIFTY POUNDS___
Date of first payment ___15 MAY 2003___ Frequency of payment ___MONTHLY___
Until ___15 APRIL 2004___ Reference ___BE/6637___
Account to be debited ___NIMRO DRAINAGE LTD___ Account number ___1203 4875___
SIGNATURE(S) ....
.... date.........................

direct debit

(a) Direct debit form completed as shown below (standing order form above).

(b) The form will be sent to Tradesure Insurance, as they will set up the payments.

(c) The direct debit will have to be signed by an authorised signatory (or two) within the business. It should also be noted that details of the due payments are normally advised by the originator of the direct debit (here the insurance company). These will be passed to the person in charge of entering up the cash book as the payments will form part of the double-entry book-keeping of the company.

—— direct debit instruction ——

Tradesure Insurance Company
PO Box 134, Helliford, HL9 6TY

Originator's Identification Number 914208
03924540234

Reference (to be completed by Tradesure Insurance) ....

Please complete the details <u>and return this form to Tradesure Insurance</u>

name and address of bank/building society
___NATIONAL BANK___
___10 CATHEDRAL STREET___
___MEREFORD___
___MR1 5DE___
account name
___NIMROD DRAINAGE LIMITED___
account number ___1203 4875___ sort code ___35.09.75___

Instructions to bank/building society
- I instruct you to pay direct debits from my account at the request of Tradesure Insurance Company
- The amounts are variable and may be debited on various dates
- I understand that Tradesure Insurance Company may change the amounts and dates only after giving me prior notice
- I will inform the bank/building society if I wish to cancel this instruction
- I understand that if any direct debit is paid which breaks the terms of this instruction, the bank/building society will make a refund.

signature(s) ___ date ___

CHAPTER 3: RECEIVING AND RECORDING PAYMENTS

3.1	Customer	Change	Notes & coin given in change
	1	£1.50	1 x £1 coin, 1 x 50p coin
	2	£6.70	1 x £5 note, 1 x £1 coin, 1 x 50p coin, 1 x 20p coin
	3	£2.49	1 x £2 coin, 2 x 20p coins, 1 x 5p coin, 2 x 2p coins
	4	£3.21	1 x £2 coin, 1 x £1 coin, 1 x 20p coin, 1 x 1p coin
	5	£0.66	1 x 50p coin, 1 x 10p coin, 1 x 5p coin, 1 x 1p coin
	6	£3.78	1 x £2 coin, 1 x £1 coin, 1 x 50p coin, 1 x 20p coin, 1 x 5p coin, 1 x 2p coin, 1 x 1p coin
	7	£7.24	1 x £5 note, 1 x £2 coin, 1 x 20p coin, 2 x 2p coins
	8	£0.58	1 x 50p coin, 1 x 5p coin, 1 x 2p coin, 1 x 1p coin
	9	£3.46	1 x £2 coin, 1 x £1 coin, 2 x 20p coins, 1 x 5p coin, 1 x 1p coin
	10	£1.92	1 x £1 coin, 1 x 50p coin, 2 x 20p coins, 1 x 2p coin

3.2

	£
cash float at start of day	28.71
plus sales made during the day	46.46
equals amount of cash held at end of day	75.17

3.3 (a) 2 x £13.99 = £27.98; 2 x 85p = £1.70; total £29.68 + VAT £5.93 = £35.61

(b) £149.95 + 99p = £150.94; add VAT of £30.18 = £181.12

(c) 2 x £35.99 = £71.98; add VAT of £14.39 = £86.37

3.4 (a) Payee name incorrect, cheque out of date, cheque not signed, amount in words and figures differs

(b) Amount in words and figures differs

(c) Out of date, amount in words and figures differs

3.5 card number, expiry date, security code

3.6 (a) £1,255.45

(b) cheque

(c) BACS, Faster Payments Service

3.7 (c)

3.8   (d)

3.9   (b)

3.10   Encryption is a method of encoding data so that payment details, eg card numbers, security codes, expiry dates – should remain secret and unavailable to hackers. The padlock symbol is displayed in sites to let customers know that sensitive data will be encrypted.

3.11   A remittance advice is a document sent to a supplier advising that money is being sent, either using a cheque (which will accompany the advice) or a BACS payment made direct to the supplier's bank account.

A remittance list is a record of items received through the post or over the counter. It is likely to include columns for the date, sender, the nature of the 'remittance' amount and the signature of the person opening the post.

CHAPTER 4: PAYING INTO THE BANK

4.1   (c)

4.2

Cheques:		Cash:		
	£20.00		2 x £20 notes	£40.00
	£18.50		5 x £10 notes	£50.00
	£75.25		8 x £5 notes	£40.00
	£68.95		2 x £1 coins	£2.00
	£182.70		6 x 50p coins	£3.00
			4 x 10p coins	£0.40
			2 x 2p coins	£0.04
				£135.44

Total amount of credit: £318.14.

4.3   Total of sales vouchers £396.94 less refund voucher £13.50, total of summary £383.44.

4.4   (a)   £2,678.90 at the beginning, £5,959.43 at the end.

(b)   3 giro credits on 10, 13, 17 November, total £1,595.30.

(c)   5 cheques on 10, 11, 21, 24, 27 November, total £1,632.27.

(d)   BACS direct credits from customers.

(e)   25 Nov Ion Power £167.50, 27 November Mercury Telecom £96.50.

(f)   £3,006.70 on 24 November through Netsales.

(g)   'DR' is short for 'debit' which in banking terms means an overdraft (the customer borrowing). If this has been the case the bank balance during the month would have gone into credit, ending up with a balance of £601.63 CR.

CHAPTER 5: BANK RECONCILIATION STATEMENTS

5.1   (a)

5.2   (c)

5.3

> **TOM REID**
>
> **BANK RECONCILIATION STATEMENT AS AT 31 DECEMBER 20-2**
>
> | | £ |
> |---|---|
> | Balance at bank as per bank statement | 207 |
> | *Less:* unpresented cheque: | |
> | B Kay (cheque no 345126) | 20 |
> | | 187 |
> | | |
> | *Add:* outstanding lodgement: | |
> | J Hill | 13 |
> | Balance at bank as per cash book | 200 |

5.4   (a)   **Cash Book** (bank columns)

20-3	Receipts		£	20-3	Payments		£
1 Jan	Balance b/d		800.50	2 Jan	A Arthur Ltd	001351	100.00
6 Jan	J Baker		495.60	9 Jan	C Curtis	001352	398.50
30 Jan	G Shotton Ltd		335.75	13 Jan	Donald & Co	001353	229.70
13 Jan	TK Supplies	BACS	716.50	14 Jan	Bryant & Sons	001354	312.00
31 Jan	Bank interest		5.50	23 Jan	P Reid	001355	176.50
				23 Jan	Omni Finance	DD	207.95
				31 Jan	Balance c/d		929.20
			2,353.85				2,353.85
1 Feb	Balance b/d		929.20				

(b)

> **P GERRARD**
>
> **BANK RECONCILIATION STATEMENT AS AT 31 JANUARY 20-3**
>
> | | £ | £ |
> |---|---|---|
> | Balance at bank as per bank statement | | 1,081.95 |
> | *Less:* unpresented cheques: | | |
> | Bryant & Sons (001354) | 312.00 | |
> | P Reid (001355) | 176.50 | |
> | | | 488.50 |
> | | | 593.45 |
> | | | |
> | *Add:* outstanding lodgement: | | |
> | G Shotton Limited | | 335.75 |
> | Balance at bank as per cash book | | 929.20 |

5.5   (a)

Cash Book (bank columns)

20-4	Receipts	£	20-4	Payments		£
1 May	Balance b/d	300	3 May	P Stone	867714	28
7 May	Cash	162	14 May	Alpha Ltd	867715	50
17 May	C Brewster	89	28 May	E Deakin	867716	110
24 May	Cash	60	17 May	Standing order: A-Z Insurance		25
28 May	Cash	40	31 May	Bank charges		10
			31 May	Balance c/d		428
		651				651
1 Jun	Balance b/d	428				

(b)

```
                    JANE DOYLE
   BANK RECONCILIATION STATEMENT AS AT 31 MAY 20-4
                                                      £
Balance at bank as per bank statement                498
Less:  unpresented cheque:
       E Deakin (867716)                             110
                                                     388
Add:   outstanding lodgement:
       cash                                           40
Balance at bank as per cash book                     428
```

5.6   (a) - (c)

CASH BOOK

Date	Details	Bank	Date	Cheque no	Details	Bank
20-5		£	20-5			£
1 May	Balance b/f	3,652	4 May	451762	Smith and Company	751
26 May	J Ackland	832	4 May	451763	Bryant Limited	268
28 May	Stamp Limited	1,119	7 May	451764	Curtis Cars	1,895
14 May	Perran Taxis	2,596	7 May	451765	Parts Supplies	1,045
			18 May		Wyvern Council	198
			20 May		A1 Insurance	1,005
			25 May		Okaro and Company	254
			25 May		Bank charges	20
			31 May		Balance c/d	2,763
		8,199				8,199
1 Jun	Balance b/d	2,763				

(d)

MILESTONE MOTORS		
Bank Reconciliation Statement as at 31 May 20-5		
	£	£
Balance at bank as per bank statement		2,707
Less: unpresented cheque no 451764		1,895
		812
Add: outstanding lodgements		
J Ackland	832	
Stamp Limited	1,119	
		1,951
Balance at bank as per cash book		2,763

5.7   (a) – (c)

CASH BOOK

Date	Details	Bank	Date	Cheque no	Details	Bank
20-8		£	20-8			£
1 Jun	Balance b/f	1,890	1 Jun	364125	Penryn Ltd	427
20 Jun	Chiverton Ltd	1,200	3 Jun	364126	Fal Boats	760
24 Jun	Perran Ltd	4,750	10 Jun	364127	S Mawes	4,200
24 Jun	P Porth	8,950	20 Jun	364128	Castle Supplies	1,062
24 Jun	*Sand & Stone*	*2,486*	*21 Jun*		*J C Property Co*	*850*
25 Jun	*Surfrider Ltd*	*4,110*	*25 Jun*		*Vord Finance*	*275*
			27 Jun		*Balance c/d*	*15,812*
		23,386				23,386
28 Jun	*Balance b/d*	*15,812*				

(d)

Bank reconciliation statement as at 27 June 20-8	
Balance as per bank statement	£ 1,672
Add	
Name: Chiverton Ltd	£ 1,200
Name: Perran Ltd	£ 4,750
Name: P Porth	£ 8,950
Name:	£
Total to add	£ 14,900
Less	
Name: Fal Boats 364126	£ 760
Name:	£
Name:	£
Name:	£
Total to subtract	£ 760
Balance as per cash book	£ 15,812

CHAPTER 6: USING CONTROL ACCOUNTS

6.1 (b)

6.2

Dr		Sales Ledger Control Account			Cr
20-7		£	20-7		£
1 Jun	Balance b/d	17,491	30 Jun	Sales returns	1,045
30 Jun	Sales	42,591	30 Jun	Bank	39,024
			30 Jun	Balance c/d	20,013
		60,082			60,082
1 Jul	Balance b/d	20,013			

6.3 (a)

Sales Ledger Control Account

Date 20-5	Details	Amount £	Date 20-5	Details	Amount £
1 Jun	Balance b/d	180,824	30 Jun	Bank	96,214
30 Jun	Sales	118,600	30 Jun	Discounts allowed	300
			30 Jun	Sales returns	650
			30 Jun	Irrecoverable debt	350
			30 Jun	Balance c/d	201,910
		299,424			299,424
1 Jul	Balance b/d	201,910			

(b)

	£
Sales ledger control account balance as at 30 June 20-5	201,910
Total of sales ledger accounts as at 30 June 20-5	202,260
Difference	350

(c) The irrecoverable debt of £350 may not have been written off in the sales ledger, and could relate to the account of Brandon Limited.

6.4 (a) **Sales ledger control account**

	Amount £	Debit ✔	Credit ✔
Balance of credit customers at 1 September 20-2	47,238	✔	
Goods sold to credit customers	31,054	✔	
Money received from credit customers	29,179		✔
Goods returned by credit customers	2,684		✔
Discounts allowed	784		✔
Irrecoverable debt written off	450		✔

(b)

£45,195	✔

(c)

£467, ie £45,195 (sales ledger control account) – £44,728 (sales ledger)

(d)

Money received from customers has been overstated in the sales ledger	✔
Sales to credit customers have been understated in the sales ledger	✔

6.5

	no action ✔	letter/email ✔	letter/email + phone call ✔
Benn Ltd		✔	
Charteris & Co	✔		
D Morgan	✔		
Wilson & Sons			✔

6.6 (c)

6.7

Dr	Purchases Ledger Control Account				Cr
20-9		£	20-9		£
30 Apr	Purchases returns	653	1 Apr	Balance b/d	14,275
30 Apr	Bank	31,074	30 Apr	Purchases	36,592
30 Apr	Set-off: sales ledger	597			
30 Apr	Balance c/d	18,543			
		50,867			50,867
			1 May	Balance b/d	18,543

6.8 (a)

Purchases Ledger Control Account

Date 20-3	Details	Amount £	Date 20-3	Details	Amount £
31 May	Bank	13,750	1 May	Balance b/d	50,300
31 May	Discounts received	500	31 May	Purchases	21,587
31 May	Purchases returns	250			
31 May	Balance c/d	57,387			
		71,887			71,887
			1 Jun	Balance b/d	57,387

(b)

	£
Purchases ledger control account balance as at 31 May 20-3	57,387
Total of purchases ledger accounts as at 31 May 20-3	56,387
Difference	1,000

(c)   There may have been a posting error and the debit balance of £500 for PP Properties may in fact be a credit balance.

6.9   (a)   Purchases ledger control account

	Amount £	Debit ✔	Credit ✔
Balance of credit suppliers at 1 August 20-4	46,297		✔
Purchases from credit suppliers	22,084		✔
Payments made to credit suppliers	25,934	✔	
Discounts received	425	✔	
Goods returned to credit suppliers	1,108	✔	

(b)

£40,914	✔

(c)

	£
Balance on purchases ledger control account at 1 September 20-4	40,914
Total of the purchases ledger balances at 1 September 20-4	39,906
Difference	1,008

(d)

A credit note was not entered in the purchases ledger control account	✔

6.10

	debit ✔	credit ✔
VAT on credit purchases	✔	
VAT on cash sales		✔
VAT on purchases returns		✔
VAT on credit sales		✔
VAT on sales returns	✔	

6.11 (a) and (b)

VAT Control Account

Date 20-4	Details	Amount £	Date 20-4	Details	Amount £
30 Jun	Purchases	4,640	30 Jun	Sales	11,200
30 Jun	Sales returns	288	30 Jun	Purchases returns	224
30 Jun	Balance c/d	6,992	30 Jun	Cash sales	496
		11,920			11,920
			1 Jul	Balance b/d	6,992

(c) Is the VAT Return correct? No

Reason: It is likely that the VAT on sales returns has been omitted from the VAT Return. The correct amount owing to HM Revenue & Customs is £6,992.

CHAPTER 7: THE JOURNAL

7.1 (c)

7.2 (b)

7.3 *financial transaction*

- opening entries for a new business
- credit purchase of goods from a supplier
- returned credit purchases to the supplier
- customer returns goods sold on credit
- BACS receipt from a customer
- credit sale of goods to a customer
- expense paid out of petty cash

book of prime entry

- journal
- purchases day book
- purchases returns day book
- sales returns day book
- cash book
- sales day book
- petty cash book

7.4

Date	Details	Reference	Dr	Cr
20-8			£	£
1 May	Vehicle	GL	6,500	
	Fixtures and fittings	GL	2,800	
	Inventory	GL	4,100	
	Bank	CB	150	
	Loan from husband	GL		5,000
	Capital*	GL		8,550
			13,550	13,550
	Assets and liabilities at the start of business			

* Assets – liabilities = capital (6,500 + 2,800 + 4,100 + 150 – 5,000 = 8,550)

7.5

Account name	Amount £	Debit ✔	Credit ✔
Cash	200	✔	
Cash at bank	2,340	✔	
Capital	*9,874*		✔
Trade payables	3,985		✔
Trade receivables	4,751	✔	
Loan from bank	12,650		✔
Office equipment	4,120	✔	
Rent paid	950	✔	
Inventory	2,310	✔	
Sundry expenses	1,194	✔	
Vehicles	8,350	✔	
Wages	2,294	✔	

Opening capital = £9,874 (assets £26,509 – liabilities £16,635)

7.6   (d)

7.7

Account name	Amount £	Debit ✔	Credit ✔
Irrecoverable debts	840	✔	
VAT	168	✔	
Sales ledger control	1,008		✔

7.8 (d)

7.9 (c)

7.10 (a)

7.11 (a) £111,650, ie £101,500 + £10,150

(b) £40,510, ie £20,500 + £9,860 + £10,150

(c) £70,290, ie £101,500 − £20,500 − £9,860 − £850

(d)

JOURNAL

Date	Details	Reference	Dr	Cr
20-3			£	£
31 Oct	Wages expense		111,650	
	Wages control			111,650
	Transfer of wages expense			

Date	Details	Reference	Dr	Cr
20-3			£	£
31 Oct	Wages control		40,510	
	HM Revenue & Customs			40,510
	Amount due to HMRC			

Date	Details	Reference	Dr	Cr
20-3			£	£
31 Oct	Wages control		70,290	
	Bank			70,290
	Net wages paid to employees			

Date	Details	Reference	Dr	Cr
20-3			£	£
31 Oct	Wages control		850	
	Trade union fees			850
	Amount due for trade union fees			

7.12   (a)

Account name	Amount £	Debit ✔	Credit ✔
Wages expense	56,110	✔	
Wages control	56,110		✔

(b)

Account name	Amount £	Debit ✔	Credit ✔
Wages control	21,105	✔	
HM Revenue & Customs	21,105		✔

(c)

Account name	Amount £	Debit ✔	Credit ✔
Wages control	32,805	✔	
Bank	32,805		✔

(d)

Account name	Amount £	Debit ✔	Credit ✔
Wages control	2,200	✔	
Pension fund	2,200		✔

CHAPTER 8: THE TRIAL BALANCE AND CORRECTION OF ERRORS

8.1

Error in the general ledger	Error disclosed by the trial balance	Error not disclosed by the trial balance
A bank payment for telephone expenses has been recorded on the debit side of both the cash book and telephone expenses account	✔	
A payment recorded in bank account for vehicle repairs has been entered in vehicles account		✔
A sales invoice has been omitted from all accounting records		✔
The balance of purchases returns account has been calculated incorrectly	✔	
A bank payment from a trade receivable has been recorded in cash book and sales ledger only	✔	
A bank payment of £85 for stationery has been recorded as £58 in both accounts		✔

8.2   (d)

8.3   (b)

8.4   (a)

8.5

Date	Details	Reference	Dr £	Cr £
(a)	Rates	GL	100	
	Rent	GL		100
(b)	Sales ledger control	GL	96	
	Sales returns	GL		96
	Sales returns	GL	69	
	Sales ledger control	GL		69

Date	Details	Reference	Dr	Cr
			£	£
(c)	Purchases ledger control	GL	175	
	Purchases returns	GL		175
	Purchases ledger control	GL	175	
	Purchases returns	GL		175
(d)	Vehicle running expenses	GL	45	
	Vehicles	GL		45

Tutorial note: for errors (b) and (c) two journal entries are required – firstly to remove the incorrect entry and, secondly, to record the correct entry.

8.6 (a) *error of omission*

Date	Details	Reference	Dr	Cr
			£	£
	Sales ledger control	GL	150	
	Sales	GL		150
	Invoice no .... omitted from the accounts: in the sales ledger – debit J Rigby £150			

(b) *error of commission*

Date	Details	Reference	Dr	Cr
			£	£
	Purchases ledger control	GL	125	
	Purchases ledger control	GL		125
	Correction of error (bank payment no ... in the purchases ledger – debit H Price Limited £125 – credit H Prince £125			

(c) *error of principle*

Date	Details	Reference	Dr	Cr
			£	£
	Delivery van	GL	10,000	
	Vehicle expenses	GL		10,000
	Correction of error – vehicle no .... invoice no .... debited to vehicle expenses in error			

(d)   *reversal of entries*

Date	Details	Reference	Dr	Cr
			£	£
	Postages	GL	55	
	Bank	CB		55
	Removing the incorrect entry: bank payment on ...(date)... for postages entered on the wrong side of both accounts			

Date	Details	Reference	Dr	Cr
			£	£
	Postages	GL	55	
	Bank	CB		55
	Recording the correct entry: bank payment on ...(date)... for postages entered on the wrong side of both accounts			

(e)   *compensating error*

Date	Details	Reference	Dr	Cr
			£	£
	Purchases	GL	100	
	Purchases returns	GL		100
	Correction of undercast on purchases account and purchases returns account on ...(date)...			

(f)   *error of original entry*

Date	Details	Reference	Dr	Cr
			£	£
	Sales ledger control	GL	98	
	Bank	CB		98
	Removing the incorrect entry: bank receipt for £89 on ...(date)... recorded as £98 instead of £89; in the sales ledger debit L Johnson £98			

Date	Details	Reference	Dr	Cr
			£	£
	Bank	CB	89	
	Sales ledger control	GL		89
	Recording the correct entry: bank receipt for £89 on ...(date)... recorded as £98 instead of £89; in the sales ledger credit L Johnson £89			

8.7

Telephone Expenses Account

Details	Amount £	Details	Amount £
Suspense	210		

Suspense Account

Details	Amount £	Details	Amount £
Balance b/d	110	Telephone expenses	210
Sales	100		

Sales Account

Details	Amount £	Details	Amount £
		Suspense	100

Vehicle Expenses Account

Details	Amount £	Details	Amount £
Vehicles	50		

Vehicles Account

Details	Amount £	Details	Amount £
		Vehicle expenses	50

8.8 (a) (i)

Account name	Amount £	Debit ✔	Credit ✔
VAT	700	✔	

(ii)

Account name	Amount £	Debit ✔	Credit ✔
VAT	800		✔

(iii)

Account name	Amount £	Debit ✔	Credit ✔
Suspense	100	✔	

(b) (i)

Account name	Amount £	Debit ✔	Credit ✔
Bank	98	✔	
Vehicle expenses	98		✔

(ii)

Account name	Amount £	Debit ✔	Credit ✔
Vehicle expenses	89	✔	
Bank	89		✔

8.9

Date	Details	Reference	Dr	Cr
			£	£
(a)	Office expenses	GL	85	
	Suspense	GL		85
	Omission of entry in office expenses account – bank payment made on ....(date)....			
(b)	Suspense	GL	78	
	Photocopying	GL		78
	Removing the incorrect entry: bank payment for photocopying £87 entered in photocopying account as £78 in error			
	Photocopying	GL	87	
	Suspense	GL		87
	Recording the correct entry: bank payment for photocopying £87 entered in photocopying account as £78 in error			
(c)	Suspense	GL	100	
	Sales returns	GL		100
	Overcast on ...(date)... now corrected			
(d)	Commission received	GL	25	
	Suspense	GL		25
	Commission received on ....(date) entered twice in commission received account, now corrected			

Dr				Suspense Account			Cr
20-4			£	20-4			£
30 Sep	Trial balance difference		19	(a)	Office expenses		85
(b)	Photocopying		78	(b)	Photocopying		87
(c)	Sales returns		100	(d)	Commission received		25
			197				197

8.10

Account name	Balances extracted on 31 December 20-4 £	Balances at 2 January 20-5	
		Debit £	Credit £
Office equipment	12,246	12,246	
Bank (cash at bank)	3,091	3,091	
Petty cash control	84	84	
Inventory	11,310	11,310	
Capital	18,246		18,246
Loan from bank	8,290		8,290
VAT owing to HM Revenue & Customs	3,105		3,105
Purchases ledger control	17,386		17,386
Sales ledger control	30,274	30,274	
Sales	82,410		82,410
Purchases	39,996	*39,496*	
Purchases returns	2,216		2,216
Sales returns	3,471	3,471	
Wages	20,212	20,212	
Advertising	4,300	*4,390*	
Insurance	1,045	1,045	
Heating and lighting	1,237	1,237	
Rent and rates	4,076	4,076	
Postages	721	721	
Suspense account (credit balance)	410		–
Totals		131,653	131,653

Tutorial note: the accounts affected by the journal entries are purchases, advertising and suspense.

8.11

Account name	Balances extracted on 30 April 20-8 £	Balances at 1 May 20-8 Debit £	Credit £
Sales	101,169		*101,269*
Sales returns	3,476	3,476	
Purchases	54,822	54,822	
Purchases returns	4,107		4,107
Sales ledger control	25,624	25,624	
Purchases ledger control	18,792		18,792
Rent and rates	3,985	3,985	
Advertising	4,867	4,867	
Insurance	1,733	1,733	
Wages	27,391	*31,246*	
Heating and lighting	3,085	3,085	
Miscellaneous expenses	107	107	
Capital	18,171		18,171
Vehicles	22,400	22,400	
Inventory	12,454	12,454	
Petty cash control	85	85	
Bank (overdraft)	6,041		*6,291*
VAT owing to HM Revenue & Customs	3,054		3,054
Loan from bank	12,200		12,200
Suspense account (debit balance)	3,505	–	
Totals		163,884	163,884

Tutorial note: the accounts affected by the journal entries are sales, wages, bank and suspense.

Index

for your notes